MARVEL STUDIOS
hawkeye

"It's time. Let's give 'em hell."

Following the events of Marvel Studios' *Avengers: Endgame*,
Clint Barton teams up with fellow archer Kate Bishop to confront his past
as the vigilante Ronin as he fights to get back to his family in time for Christmas.

THE OFFICIAL MARVEL STUDIOS SPECIALS

Thor: Ragnarok
Black Panther
Black Panther: The Official Movie Companion
Marvel Studios: The First 10 Years
Avengers: Infinity War
Ant-Man and The Wasp
Captain Marvel
Avengers: Endgame
Avengers: An Insider's Guide to the Avengers Films
Black Widow
WandaVision
The Falcon and The Winter Soldier
Loki
Eternals
Spider-Man: No Way Home
Doctor Strange in the Multiverse of Madness

TITAN EDITORIAL
Editor Jonathan Wilkins
Group Editor Jake Devine
Art Director Oz Browne
Assistant Editor Calum Collins
Copy Editor Matt McAllister
Production Controller Kelly Fenlon
Production Controller Caterina Falqui
Production Manager Jackie Flook
Sales and Circulation Manager Steve Tothill
Marketing Coordinator Lauren Noding
Publicity and Sales Coordinator Alexandra Iciek
Publicity Manager Will O'Mullane
Digital and Marketing Manager Jo Teather
Acquisitions Editor Duncan Baizley
Publishing Directors Ricky Claydon
& John Dziewiatkowski
Group Operations Director Alex Ruthen

Executive Vice President Andrew Sumner
Publishers Vivian Cheung & Nick Landau

DISTRIBUTION
U.S. Newsstand: Total Publisher Services, Inc.
John Dziewiatkowski, 630-851-7683
U.S. Newsstand Distribution: Curtis Circulation Company

PRINTED IN CHINA

U.S. Bookstore Distribution: The News Group
U.S. Direct Sales: Diamond Comic Distributors

For more info on advertising contact
adinfo@titanemail.com

Marvel Studios' Hawkeye The Official Collector Special
published May 2023 by Titan Magazines, a division of

Titan Publishing Group Limited, 144 Southwark Street,
London, SE1 0UP.
For sale in the U.S. and Canada.
ISBN: 9781787734722

Thanks to, Kevin Pearl, Samantha Keane, Rodney Vallo,
Shiho Tilley, and Eugene Paraszczuk at Disney.

TITAN MAGAZINES **MARVEL**
© 2023 MARVEL

MARVEL STUDIOS

hawkeye

CONTENTS

04 **JEREMY RENNER**
– Clint Barton / Hawkeye

12 **HAILEE STEINFELD**
– Kate Bishop

20 **FLORENCE PUGH**
– Yelena Belova

26 **TONY DALTON**
– Jack Duquesne

30 **VERA FARMIGA**
– Eleanor Bishop

34 **THE "TRACKSUIT MAFIA"**
– Aleks Paunovic, Carlos Navarro,
and Piotr Adamczyk

38 **ALAQUA COX**
– Maya Lopez / Echo

44 **VINCENT D'ONOFRIO**
– Wilson Fisk / Kingpin

50 **FRA FEE**
– Kazi Kazimierczak

52 **AVA RUSSO**
– Lila Barton

54 **ROGERS THE MUSICAL!**
– Jason MacDonald, Ty Adam,
Tom Feeney, Nico Dejesus,
Meghan Manning,
Marc Shaiman,
Josh Bergasse,
Harris Matthew Turner,
Adam Pascal

58 **THE LARPERS**
– Clayton English,
Adelle Drahos, and
Adetinpo Thomas

62 **FIGHTS**
– Adam Lytle, Heidi Moneymaker,
and Noon Orsatti

68 **CHOREOGRAPHY**
– Katherine Rotary

70 **PRODUCTION DESIGN**
– Maya Shimoguchi

76 **COSTUME**
– Michael Crow

82 **WRITER**
– Heather Quinn

86 **PRODUCERS**
– Trinh Tran and
Brad Winderbaum

92 **DIRECTORS**
– Bert & Bertie, and
Rhys Thomas

JEREMY RENNER

HAWKEYE

A stalwart of the Marvel Cinematic Universe since his first appearance in Marvel Studios' *Thor,* for more than a decade Jeremy Renner has battled the bad guys be it as an Avenger or a vigilante. Here, he discusses taking up his bow and arrow once more for the latest chapter in Hawkeye's evolution...

Could you have ever imagined this journey in the Marvel Cinematic Universe?
I'm not that imaginative—I don't think anybody really could be. I always had pretty high hopes for Marvels' *The Avengers,* seeing the success of what Robert Downey, Jr. had done and Marvel Studios' *Iron Man* back in those days, and that's why I decided to jump on. But to see where it's gone— it feels like it's gone in a flash but then also been a big part of my life for so long. The best takeaway from all of this is the wonderful friendships established over the last decade. I had relationships with a handful of [my co-stars] prior to shooting, but our friendships grew because a lot of big things happened in our lives personally that we got to share together.

Marvel Studios put us in the position to have a long storytelling form in cinema, and it's just mind-boggling to see how that's come together—by happenstance, a lot of luck, a lot of talent, a lot of support, and a lot of work. It's something that we all get to share together. I remember putting all our hands in the cement with [Kevin] Feige. That was such a wonderful honor to think how far we had come and how well everything has turned out for everyone involved in the MCU.

Is there a lot of dramatic breadth to Clint Barton?
I think in Marvel Studios' *Avengers: Age of Ultron,* when they cemented the family life, that was a huge thing for the original six Avengers. It just became what they were doing it all for. Clint had family and kids and was changing diapers while still slinging arrows. I had to redefine in my head what a Super Hero is and what a super power really is.

Slowly discovering Clint and finally getting to spend a lot of time with him has been a big learning process for me. There is a lot of information and a lot of stuff going on in this show, so there was a lot to learn. I did try to find his voice and sense of humor and the timing of his life, instead of just quippy lines here and there and some arrows and fighting. It was a wonderful way to just really dig and discover a lot more of the humanity of who Clint Barton is. I'm very blessed for that.

How have the days of Ronin affected Clint?
That ties in with the Blip when he lost his family. He took his pain and rage and sadness and everything out on every bad guy on the planet. It was a giant weight and burden because he knew he was going outside the moral code of what he is. It's something he's had to carry with him, but he also carried the death of his entire family and pretty much everyone else. Everyone dealt with those losses in a different way, and he just became a vigilante. When everything was wiped clean and everybody came back, he was still carrying that weight. And that's what we start tying into this series: things that happen in the past catch up to you.

Was the chemistry between you and Hailee Steinfeld instantly established?
I've known her for a while, but she's grown up a lot now. She was 13 when I first met her, and now she's a young woman. I took on the role of shepherding her into how Marvel Studios works with all the stunts and the chaos of schedules, and she just fell into trust with me because I was looking after her in those ways and trying to protect her as much as I possibly could. I have absolute respect, love, admiration, and trust in her. When you have that, I feel like true art can then exist because you have trust with one another. Whenever there was an obstacle, we would try to help each other through. ▶

Does Kate give Clint hope?
I think he sees a lot in her. At first, she's a real pain in the butt and then becomes a real problem, but then he learns to have a lot of respect and adoration for her, and then teaches her and protects her and eventually [they] work together. The intersection of those two characters becomes, really, the big base of what this show is about. I felt like our chemistry really popped off the screen. I was really excited to see how that fully came together.

Would you say that they have a very astute father/daughter relationship?
For sure. I think it was pretty natural and we didn't have to work very hard at that. But [Hailee's] a very talented actress. She's wonderful to work with and very fluid. I didn't really have to act too hard with her.

How did Florence Pugh stand in for what you had been used to with Scarlett Johansson?
She was game. She's a great collaborator and was wonderful to work with. There were a lot of issues that we had to work through story-wise, because she was tying in what happened in Marvel Studios' *Black Widow*. So we just had to figure out how to tie it together and make it make sense, because [our characters] didn't know each other. We were trying to fill in the holes of truths and back story. She was really wonderful to help

01 Jeremy Renner returns as Hawkeye.

02 Renner was pleased for the opportunity to explore Clint Barton's humanity.

03 The show focusses on the relationship between Barton and his protégé Kate Bishop.

04 With an arsenal of variant arrows, Renner had fun filming the high-powered action sequences.

04

"You can get very creative with what an arrow tip can do and we were all chiming in with different ideas."

shape that and we had some writers on set, too, so [we could] figure that out really quickly.

How did you find the addition of the arrow tech for this show?
Kevin [Feige] was really into the idea of using a bunch of different trick arrowheads and tips that could do different things. You can get very creative on what an arrow tip can do and we were all chiming in with different ideas. It really helped with the spectacle of making it cinematic.

The arrows really came into their own during the car chase sequence. How much fun was that to film?
I was just rolling through the streets of New York—Atlanta doubling for New York—and it was pretty fun. I remember they had this rig that they put the car on. It was an amazing thing where the stunt driver could get on top of it and was able to drive us around through the streets. We were in the car, they put cameras everywhere, and he could drive from any position. We were doing donuts, going 60 miles an hour, doing 180s and just anything that a stunt driver would do. It allowed us the freedom to feel comfortable in the car, and we could do what we needed to do. It made it pretty fun doing it that way. I'd never done that before. ▶

05

▶ **Does that approach really change the acting?**
It really felt like you were a part of and in it. Both
Hailee and I—our jaws were on the floor, because you
never get to experience that. Usually, it's driving 25
miles an hour and we're just pretending to drive fast or
whatever it might be. We were living in it like it was a
roller coaster ride or something. We just loved it. When
you're in it and it's real and it's all around you, that's a
pretty exhilarating experience.

**How was the physicality of the role and embracing that
side of things?**
We had Heidi Moneymaker—who I've worked with
[before] because she played Black Widow as the stuntie
—and she was able to do all the fight stuff and all the
stunt coordinating. Stylistically, that's also part of what
Clint Barton looks like when he fights. There are a lot
of characteristics that come from the stunt department,
which is very, very, very important to the storytelling,
especially in the MCU. We were so, so fortunate to have
her on this.

How was working with Alaqua Cox?
Let's talk about Alaqua. Alaqua has never acted before.
She's deaf. She's amazing. It's a different experience
trying to [act] when you're working with someone who
is deaf, because there are a lot of different things that
have to go on for her to know and understand. And
then never acting before was a little tricky, but she's
a wonderful, wonderful human. She really knocked it
out of the park. It's a very physical role and she just did
everything, She was just really wide open emotionally ▶

06

05 Clint Barton shows
a suaver side as he
and Kate take a break
from the action.

06 Barton is reunited
with his daughter, Lila.

07 Barton dons his
iconic purple and
black field suit.

▶ and was able to contribute a lot. She was tremendous. She was such a delight to work with. I think she's going to do well, and I love the turn of her character. I'm pretty excited to see what happens in the future.

What about Clint's hearing loss?

To get more true to the comics, we introduce that Clint [as a result of] explosions and all those things, has become hard of hearing in one ear and has a hearing aid. It was a good thing to get back into, because it was an original comic thing. To be able to implement that in the show was really awesome.

Was it intentional to make this a more grounded story?

Yeah, it's a very grounded world that they're in right now. Of course, there are always options for it to go galactic anytime—as soon as some spaceship lands—but you just never know, and that's the beauty of the MCU. It could just go anywhere. But when you're learning about Clint Barton more, and learning about [his] back story and history, having a grounded world is a better canvas for that to happen.

It also makes sense, because everything that happened from the years of Ronin are catching back up with him. All the bad guys are coming back to get him when Ronin appears again. So it all makes sense. It would be weird if it was on Vormir or in a spaceship.

Are there a lot of emotional connections at play?

[Clint's] being held accountable for actions, whether they were justified or not. It's still the effects of Ronin killing William Lopez—Maya's father. I let her know it was me and have to apologize and explain that her dad was a bad guy. And the same with Yelena. We've never met, and all she wants to do is kill me because she heard I killed her sister. So it was another similar scenario where [I have to explain] I didn't kill her. There's a wonderful, deep connection that we end up having because we both share one of the greatest losses of our lives from losing Natasha. It's pretty haunting.

What has this journey meant to you?

It's hard to quantify what it's meant for me in my career, outside of it has certainly made me famous. When a fourth grader and third grader knows your first and last name, that's a strange thing. But when I think of the MCU and my experiences playing this character in every film that I was fortunate enough to be able to do, it becomes much more of a personal journey than how it has affected my career. It's been much more [about] looking at the wonderful relationships I've got to forge. When you do a film, usually you're done and you move on. [But] this is a lot of films, so you get to have that family element and continue on through so many years. To have careers shared together—they are very, very far and few between, and I feel very blessed for that. That's what I think about when I think about my time in the MCU. ☻

08 Barton is forced to confront the dark days when he went under the name "Ronin".

09 Barton and Kate Bishop following another action-filled escapade.

10 A seasonal scene as Hawkeye gets into gift-giving mode.

HAILEE STEINFELD

KATE BISHOP

From archery lessons to hand-to-hand combat, Hailee Steinfeld reveals how she had to do some straight shooting to bring fan favorite character Kate Bishop to life.

How exciting was it to come into the Marvel Cinematic Universe in this role?
When I got the call that I was being asked to join the MCU, I had just showed up to work on another job—I was literally [about to get] out the car, and I saw the call coming in. I just started crying. I was so overcome with emotions, I didn't really know what to think. I was obviously very excited, very honored, thrilled, but [also] terrified.

It's an honor to be a part of the MCU, and as Kate Bishop, nonetheless. She's an incredible, incredible thing, and to bring her to life in ways that people know and love from the comics is really exciting.

What did they tell you about the character and the series?
I didn't know much about Kate Bishop other than fans were very excited about her story being brought to life. From there, I just dove right in. It's always so fun to play a character that has all of this preexisting information. So, I was very excited to meet with the team and hear what they were thinking.

It was a really fun process to figure out who she is, her voice, and what she looks like. She's a young woman growing up in New York City, and she's got a lot of wit. She's very brave, charismatic, sometimes annoying—but very skilled – and ultimately a very fun person to be around. She's a really fun person to get to know and to play.

How would you describe Kate?
She is ultimately the kind of person that wants to see people smile. She wants to help people and she wants to make people feel good, and if it means putting herself in somewhat of a compromising situation, she'll do it. She knows that she's smart enough to get out of it or get around it.

How much training did you have for the role?
Everything happened very quickly from the time that I got the call to the time that I showed up [on set] ready to shoot. I don't know the exact amount of time, but it wasn't a lot. I had a few archery lessons with an amazing coach in Los Angeles. The first handful of lessons were spent really just talking and being taught the mechanics of the bow: how to hold it and how to change the limbs. The whole technical side of things is what I was introduced to first, which I'm so grateful for, but at the time I was like, "dude, I really just want to shoot." But I'm so thankful to know the in's and out's of it, because once all that information is stored, you can place it in the back of your head and know that it's there, and it becomes more and more second nature after tons of repetition. I had a few sessions in LA, then I went out to Atlanta and I started working with the bow in a different way, and that was through stunt training.

First of all, a bow is a weapon without any arrows, and learning how to fight with just that was a whole thing in itself. Before I went out to Atlanta to shoot, I was also training in LA on the stunt side of things with my dad, who is a personal trainer. We spent months on all sorts of different styles of fighting and hand-to-hand combat. Once I had my first archery lesson, we started getting into exercises and circuits of training that would help me with those muscles because, let me tell you, if you've never shot a bow and arrow before, you are sore in places you never knew you could be sore the next day. It's something that looks so beautiful and so effortless, but it is so hard. There were plenty of scenes where I was just holding it up for a while, and by the end of the take, my arm was shaking and my neck was hurting. It requires a lot more strength than it looks. ▶

"Finding the banter between Clint and Kate came pretty naturally."

▶ **Does stunt training always come naturally to you?**
I love that this role is very physical. I've always been into training my body and any sort of physical activity. I love that this job left me no excuse but to get to a place where I can be shown something—whether it was right before a take or months in advance—and I would be able to pick it up quickly. But that didn't just happen, I definitely had to prep for that.

Was it nice to be working alongside Jeremy Renner, who has so much knowledge of the MCU?
It was so fun doing this thing with Jeremy. I remember meeting him when I was about 13 years old, so it was cool to be with him over a decade later, working on [Marvel Studios' *Hawkeye*]. I remember sitting down with him for the first time on this project and really getting right into it. Right away I felt this sense of comfort, knowing that this is a world he has been in for ten years. Knowing that I was going into this for the first time with somebody who knew the lay of the land was very comforting. He was so supportive in showing me the ropes and collaborating with me in finding this amazing dynamic between Clint and Kate. It was fun.

How did you find the dynamic with Jeremy?
Finding the banter between Clint and Kate came pretty naturally, and it does feel quite similar to the banter that

I have with Jeremy. You see posters of Hawkeye in Kate's childhood bedroom, so he is generally somebody she has idolized for a very long time and there is very much a part of her that is marveling over the fact that he's right in front of her, and that they're walking down the street, having a casual conversation. Then there are moments where she is very aware of what she's capable of. She knows she can prove him wrong in certain aspects, and she knows that she can keep up with him, and I think that he sees that too. There are maybe moments where he doesn't want to believe it or have anything to do with any of it, but there's a real connection between the two of them where, through it all, they see each other's capabilities. We're talking about two people who are highly skilled and highly trained in what they do, but they're humans and it's all human strength. So I think at the end of the day, they can look at each other and see that they're both humans going through these crazy situations, and that they are the only ones that are going to get them through.

How was it playing opposite Vera Farmiga (Eleanor Bishop)?
Vera is so incredible and so kind and patient. That was a really fun relationship and dynamic to play out—to be so suspect of your own mother. [Kate has] devoted her entire life to protecting her and then realizes she has been protecting somebody who is hurting humanity. It's the complete opposite of who Kate is and what she stands for.

01 Kate Bishop suits up for the final battle.

02 Hailee Steinfeld goes before the camera during the filming of an action set piece.

03 Steinfeld was pleased to shoot scenes in New York, one of her favorite places in the world.

04 Kate gains the upper hand when she duels Jack Duquesne, her mother's fiancé.

05 Kate joins forces with Clint Barton. (Overleaf)

03

How great was it working with the rest of the cast?

It's so awesome to be not only a part of this world, but a part of this world with some really amazing people and some really talented actors. [The show] was such a fun experience all the way around, and I'm so grateful to have experienced it with Jeremy, Vera [Farmiga, Eleanor Bishop], Tony [Dalton, Jack Duquesne] and Florence [Pugh, Yelena]. It was so fun.

When Florence and I had our first day together, I just remember being so excited about the fact that there was another female that came onto the set and totally took ownership of her space and her character, and who she is in our story. Florence has such an incredible energy. As a fan of hers, I was very excited to meet her and so happy that we had a genuinely good time together. Yelena is such an amazing character.

How was filming in New York?

New York is one of my favorite places in the world. It's just so unique and so special. The energy there can't be replicated. You go to New York and you know you're in New York; you go into the city, and you know you're in the city. And you go during Christmas time, and it's really unlike anything else.

As part of developing Kate—her wardrobe, her attitude and mannerisms—New York was a really big thing for me. I have spent more time there in my life in the last few years than ever before. I would by no means in any way ever consider myself a local or a New Yorker, but you definitely walk with a different purpose there. I just really wanted to have New York be as much a part of Kate as it is a part of those who are born and raised there. ▶

04

"As crazy, wild, and surreal as the show might feel at times, it is very human."

▶ **What was it like to get the costume?**

I was so excited about the whole Super Hero costume element of joining the MCU. When it came time to have one of my first fittings, I didn't really know what to expect, but I was very excited. I walked into the room and they had all the references up on the wall of the many versions of Kate's Super Hero look. I was just so eager to find out what we were going to land on.

The costume wasn't going to [come into] play until the end of our shoot, so it was being built in LA, and at one point during the middle of the shoot, it arrived in Atlanta. We had a fitting and a bunch of changes needed to be made, so they sent it back to LA. Then there was this whole question of whether it was going to make it back in time, which put everybody under pressure.

It was awesome to see the final product of her costume come to life, especially knowing that Kate has a version of this suit that she makes. The whole time we were calling it the homemade Hawkeye suit, and then it just became something so official and so clean and so, so good. I love it.

Does putting it on make you feel different?

Oh yeah! The under layers of these things need to be talked about more because the amount of snaps, zippers, Velcro bits and the hook and eyes and all that, is mad. But it definitely, definitely affects your physicality, for better or for worse. Sometimes they're a little tight in certain places, but it definitely helps get you into the mindset.

How would you sum up the story?

As crazy, wild and surreal as the show might feel at times, it is very human. It feels very real and very raw. It's very rooted in family and emotional beings going through life and trying to make it through certain challenges, that they either have to prove to themselves they can get through on their own, or that they need somebody to get through it with. It's just a very real and honest story at the end of the day, but still very wild and still very fun.

How was the whole experience and how excited are you for the future?

Whatever the future holds, I just feel very lucky to be a part of something, and to be a part of the MCU of all things. It's truly an honor. I had an amazing time and I'm excited to see what happens. ☻

06 Steinfeld feels that
the series is a "very
real and honest story."

07 Kate and
Lucky the Pizza
Dog encounter
Clint Barton.

08 Kate Bishop dons
the Ronin costume in
an effort to get Clint
Barton's attention...

09 ...but instead finds
the unwanted
attention of the
Tracksuit Mafia.

FLORENCE PUGH

YELENA BELOVA

Having made her debut as Yelena, the late Natasha Romanoff's younger 'sister' in Marvel Studios' *Black Widow*, Florence Pugh is no stranger to the Marvel Cinematic Universe. Reprising her character for *Hawkeye*, the actor discusses some of the transformations her character has undergone since we last saw her...

What did you want Yelena to be for her return?
I think from the get-go on Marvel Studios' *Black Widow*, I was really awarded the space and the opportunity and the freedom to create a new character, and that was totally down to director Cate Shortland. As exciting as it is to come into these big films, you're always interested and wanting to know how much freedom you have with these characters. I was just so amazed and excited that Cate was like, "Look, this is yours. It's going to go to you. You're going to continue this character, and you make it essentially whatever you want it to be." That was just so exciting and thrilling for me. So I've always wanted Yelena to be that she has kind of an unexpected edge to her. You don't really know whether she's going to be in a great mood, or a [bad] mood.

I wanted her to be a bit odd and for her timing to be unnatural. I think that's something that makes her quite lovable because she's just this incredibly inter-changing character. Coming into this series, knowing what we had done with Marvel Studios' *Black Widow* and knowing where I'd come from, that was an amazing gift to be given. And then, of course, in terms of story line, the difference of Marvel Studios' *Black Widow* to this is miles away because she's a changed person now.

How did you approach where she's been since *Black Widow*?
I think when we finished *Black Widow* I knew in the back of my head that if this character was asked to come back, [she] would be a completely different person because the whole film, the whole storyline of *Black*

Widow, is that she's got her sister back and she's found her family again.

I knew going into that film that Natasha didn't make it back into her life, so from the get-go, I was automatically thinking about where [Yelena's] mind was at. How does she find out [about Natasha's death]? Who tells her? How does she react? Who does she go after? I did not see it coming that they were going to put me and Clint against each other, which I thought was a really cool twist. So, I think in my head I'd already done the planning. I was really happy to have such a raw and painful revenge.

It was fascinating to be – in my character's head – a good person, but to everybody else, she is bad. That was an interesting line to walk.

What can you tell us about her look for the show?
One thing that has been really wonderfully translated into this series is that she still wears the same suit – it's just a different color. One thing I really wanted with Yelena was that I didn't want her to be in tight suits. I didn't want her to be a silhouette. I wanted her to be in clothes that she could fight in that was a different look to what we've seen before. I was really happy with the suit that I wore in *Black Widow*. I could actually do all of my stunts, which was such a win, and to my surprise, they made a black one for this series, which was just so exciting. So, for me, I'm really happy that her look stayed the same.

We also had some amazing hair and makeup opportunities for the final episode, which are another wink at just how weird Yelena's personality is. I really loved the idea that she gets dressed up to kill her enemy; that she really makes an effort to do awesome hair, put on ▶

"Yelena really comes in with one purpose —she doesn't hang about."

▶ lipstick and blue mascara, because she's reveling in the idea that she is going to kill the man that killed her sister. To me, that is pure Yelena's humor.

I also did a scene playing a tourist in New York, and I said to Dennis, who is head of makeup, [that maybe] Yelena is having a practical joke and her version of humor is that she essentially has the blueprint of who she is on her nails. So, on my nails I have the black widow sign on two, and then on another two I have the Russian flag, and then on my thumbs I have a knife, and I have a web. I had an amazing nail lady that did them called Vanessa. I just wanted it to be her joke that she's pretending to be a tourist. She's undercover, but she has done her nails with exactly who she is underneath. That's Yelena. She does her own jokes to make herself laugh.

Did you enjoy working on the action sequences with Jeremy Renner?
I was very excited to come on board. I'm only in a few episodes and Yelena really comes in with one purpose—she doesn't hang about. One of the scenes that I was excited to do was that confrontation scene. When they told me that I was going to be in Marvel Studios' *Hawkeye* and that Yelena was out to kill Clint, I knew that there was going to be that confrontation scene at some point, so I was happy to know that it was going to go hand in hand with a big stunt sequence. For about five days before that scene I was in the stunts warehouse, and we were just figuring out where it would be best to have each beat of the fight. It was just really cool to be involved with that.

Then, of course, when I actually got to do it with Jeremy, he was very emotional about the scene that he did with Scarlett all those years ago. I think he was a bit intimidated by this scene because my character calls him out on it. It's very painful, and I think what we shot was perfect and raw. It shows two broken people—broken for the same reason – coming face to face, and having to understand and move on with what Natasha decided to do.

In that fight, Jeremy tells me that he didn't kill her—she made that decision. I really wanted that to mean something else to Yelena; the thought that Natasha left her again—the thought that she chose to jump over the edge again... What would that make her do? That would make her act out. And if [Clint] was the last person to see her, he was the one that could have prevented her from dying. So then I blame him for not jumping over the edge before her. There are lots of different stages in that fight. Jeremy was so fun to work with and so easy to go there with and was just rough and ready, and as ready to bruise as I was.

01 Florence Pugh as Yelena Belova.

02 Stalking Hawkeye during the season finale.

03 Yelena finds herself face to face with Hawkeye.

04 From left: Executive producer Trinh Tran, Hailee Steinfeld, Florence Pugh, and directors Bert & Bertie.

I felt very lucky to do that confrontation scene with him, because that's the crux—that's the crescendo of that storyline. I felt very grateful to be a part of the making of it.

How was working with Hailee [Steinfeld]?
My first day of shooting was my biggest scene with her, and I was really grateful that it was that scene that I started on because I felt so welcomed. It's very intimidating joining a shoot that's been going for months with so many actors and members of the crew, so to come in on a scene like that and really establish who I am and everybody being so welcoming, was so wonderful.

Then, of course, my relationship with Hailee is like our little heartbeat throughout both of our stories. They're both craving friendship—especially Yelena— and I think even though [Kate] is connected to Clint, [Yelena] feels that she's not the real issue. And she also has that lovely idea that if they really fought, [Yelena] would win in two seconds.

So, Yelena figures she may as well have a friend in all of this, and I think that's kind of sweet. You can see that Yelena is desperately craving that friendship. I only got to shoot with Hailee for a few days, but we definitely got some fun stuff in there.

04

"If I had slid by an inch, I would have properly clocked Jeremy in the face!"

▶ **How was the new weapon?**
I had the baton before in Marvel Studios' *Black Widow*, but the single baton—no, that was the first time, which was awesome. That was such a big feature of the fight.

What was it like to work on that ice rink during the climactic showdown?
It was very, very slippy. It was almost like the material on the air hockey that you play at arcades. It was that, basically, which is great if you're pretending to slide around, but if you're having to do really precise fighting, it is absolutely terrifying. Stunts figured out the solution and they got a white carpet to put down when we were fighting, but there were a couple of times where I had to do a take where I wasn't on the carpet. That was just so scary, because if I had slid even by an inch, I would have properly clocked Jeremy in the face. When you're doing stunts, you have to know that you're not going to get anyone and that you're never going to catch them in the face, and that's down to your placement and their placement. When you are standing on faux ice and you're skidding around all over the place, the likelihood of you hitting someone just increases completely. So that was a little bit sketchy, but we figured it out. It actually made parts of the fight really fun and interesting because you did slide, and you would have to move. You wouldn't have been able to have got that effect any other way.

Is it nice to have that practicality?
Totally—and I really like that, especially with the way that filmmaking is going. I've been on a couple of things in the last few years where people are going back to locations and are using the real place. I have to say I really appreciate that, especially with the ice rink. Actually, all of the office stuff, when we did the office fight with Kate, was on a real location. It just means that it's all real and you're not having to act, which is the biggest gift to give someone.

Was it fun to shoot the flashback scene?
Yeah, and I think going forward, we're going to find out more about Yelena. It's so tricky covering those beats when they're such huge beats, and I think the evolution of Yelena, from where we met her in Marvel Studios' *Black Widow* to here, is that so much has happened in those years. She's found out a lot, so of course, it's lovely to fill in the blanks, but it's also really tricky to only just tell 20 seconds of her timeline when they are probably the biggest 20 seconds of her life. It's always hard when you're only given a smidgen to cover so much ground. But maybe we'll see more of that era. I don't know. ☻

05 Yelena meets Clint Barton's protégé, Kate Bishop.

06 Pugh films the action-packed ice rink fight on the blue screen set.

07 Filming the action scenes made for a fun experience for Pugh.

08 Pugh enjoyed exploring Yelena's character in the flashback sequence.

TONY DALTON

JACK DUQUESNE

Tony Dalton plays Jack Duquesne, the charming but shady new fiancé of Eleanor Bishop. The actor reveals more about fencing lessons, researching the Marvel comic books, and bringing out the different sides of the character.

Were you a fan of the Marvel Cinematic Universe before this?

I mean, who isn't a fan of these movies? They're great. They're for the whole family, they did a great job doing them, and they're a huge success. They're all over the world and they're part of our culture. I wouldn't go as far as to say that I was a diehard fan, but I was definitely a fan. When I got the call and they told me about this whole project, I was very excited.

Did you like the fact that it was a six-episode series?

I like that it was six hours because it gives you a little more chance to dig deeper into the character and to maybe show different sides of a character. It's longer storytelling, so [audiences] have more time to really get into it. And the action scenes were really something else. They threw everything at this.

How fun was it to shoot in New York?

Are you kidding me, man? I used to live here. I was a waiter here for five years. Coming back and working for Marvel Studios and hanging out with those fine fellas, and that Christmas tree, and working on what I love, it was a blessing, man.

Was this the first time you've fenced?

I actually did take fencing back in the day when I was in New York in the '90s. I took a couple of semesters back in college. For some reason, I was drawn to fencing. It came in handy! So I kinda knew what I was doing, but I needed to refresh my memory. It had been a long time. When I got the part, I got myself a professional fencer, and we went at it for weeks, just to get the gist of it. I mean, this guy [Jack] has got swords all over the place.

I figured I might as well get ahead. Thank God I did, 'cause otherwise it would've looked like I didn't know what I was doing, you know? But it was kinda like riding a bicycle. You remember the moves, the stance and stuff. It definitely helped.

They also had stunt [people] for the parts where the sword goes close to the face. With the stunt person, you can go all out!

How did it feel wearing the fencing outfit?

It's like pajamas, man. It's like a onesie. It's delicious. You just fall right asleep in your trailer while you're waiting.

Fencing is a sport that seems to suit Jack.

It's very elegant. It's very grand. I like it because the character is very much like that, so they go hand in hand. He's got this whole sort of class about him. And fencing has that. It seems like a very classy sport.

How would you describe Jack?

He's this dapper personality, and the new fiancé. These rich guys live in this huge penthouse up in the sky, so life is good for him right now. But you're not too sure about this guy. You don't know what's going on with him.

The first time you see him he's got this rose between his teeth, and he's kind of like, "Ta-da!" He's a little bit clownish. But you never know if he's playing the clown or if he really is [like] that. You don't know if this guy is putting on a show or not.

Can you talk about his dynamic with Kate?

Kate doesn't like him, obviously, for the reason that there's a new man in the family coming in, but also because he's sort of shady. As far as Jack's concerned, Kate's just a little girl who's not happy because there's a new guy in ▶

02

"Jack is a sort of swashbuckler kind of Errol Flynn type of character."

01 Suave swordsman Jack Duquense as played by Tony Dalton.

02 Jack lends his fiancé, Eleanor, his jacket.

03 Kate Bishop has a frosty relationship with her stepfather to be.

04 Fresh out of jail. Duquesne attends the Bishop family Christmas party.

05 Ready for action in his fencer's uniform.

▶ the house. He doesn't really care about her. With time, he starts maybe connecting more with her, but at first she's non-existent to him. It's just like, "Oh, OK, so the daughter doesn't like me. Of course she doesn't like me." It's that kind of dynamic.

Was it tricky to balance the clownish and shady aspects of the character?
I mean, it's hard to get the tone because tone is always very specific. You don't want to overdo it, and also you don't want to underdo it. But Rhys Thomas and Bert & Bertie, the directors, and Trinh, the producer, really set me in the right direction of how much I could be foolish and then [show] at the same time that the guy is a master swordsman. He's not that dumb, you know what I mean?

Did you do much research into the comic book character?
I did, just to get a quick glimpse of it. As a matter of fact my brother, when I told him about this part, got me all these comic books about the Swordsman that were printed all those years back. So I just kind of got into it, seeing what this guy was like and what [comics character] he was created around. Jack is a sort of swashbuckler, kind of Errol Flynn type of character. I tried to instill that a little bit into the character—this very debonair, very classy kind of guy, you know?

How did you find working with Vera Farmiga?
Vera is amazing, man. She's so cool to work with, and we hit it off. There's one scene where I had to twirl her around and dance with her. I was so worried about that because I didn't want to look like an idiot. And she said, "Don't worry about it. We're going to do just fine." So we rehearsed it a little, I twirled her around and set her on the sofa, and we kept doing the scene. It was great fun. It was great working with her.

How about working with Jeremy Renner and Hailee Steinfeld?
Working with Jeremy's amazing. I've been a fan of his work for a long time, and he's a great guy. And Hailee is such a nice person to work with. She's such a sweet girl. She was always smiling on the set and she was always nice to everybody. Setting that tone to work around is always really nice. [When you're] around actors that are just nice to each other, it's going to work out perfectly.

The shoot involved a lot of hard work, didn't it?
A lot of people worked really hard to get this done. We worked nights for weeks. Everybody gets tired, but everybody was so excited. You get out there and you do it, and then you just kinda sit back and wait and see how people enjoy it. ◉

03

04

05

VERA FARMIGA

ELEANOR BISHOP

Vera Farmiga plays Eleanor Bishop, the wealthy CEO of a successful security firm and mother to the arrow-slinging Kate. Yet despite her money and success, Eleanor harbors some murky secrets...

What were your thoughts on entering the Marvel Cinematic Universe?
To be honest, I had never seen a single Marvel Studios [show]. I had no idea what I was getting into. I had no idea how massive the universe was and what a massive fanbase [it had]... And so I ended up, one by one, going through all the films. Then it dawned on me how neat it was to have received that invitation. I was psyched, man! I saw these extraordinary actors having a blast with their characters and with each other.

How would you sum up the character of Eleanor Bishop?
Kate's mom, Eleanor—not unlike an Avenger —is in the business of keeping people safe. It's her particular life experience that drew her into the work of security. She sees her work as a kind of heroicism, protecting people, keeping them safe. One day she hopes that she'll be able to hand down the keys of the Bishop Security dynasty to her daughter —and that may not be Kate's vision.

How would you describe the relationship between Eleanor and Kate?
Our story is grounded in the human side of the MCU. Eleanor has been single-handedly raising Kate for over a decade. Eleanor and Kate sometimes butt heads, [and] I think the reason for that is that they're quite similar. Both women are confident, capable, strong-willed and opinionated. And yet they're very different. Kate has been handed everything in her life. She has been born into a lavish life. Whereas, Eleanor came from nothing. She had to work for everything. So those differing experiences really informed their character traits. Kate is very confident but cavalier. Eleanor is confident but very cautious.

Bottom line, though: I think Eleanor is a good mama bear, and has got that umbilical cord wrapped around her daughter. I think her North Star is to protect her and to guide her as she sees that she's so full of potential. [She wants] to protect her from ever feeling as vulnerable as Eleanor has felt in her life. And she has a vision of success for Kate that Kate may not agree with.

We all know that mother/daughter dynamics can be complicated. It's hard work raising a successful daughter, especially if the two of you have very different definitions of what that success means. Those dynamics are in our story. They play out in a really complex way. We explore the pendulum swing of love and conflict that comes with a young woman who's growing up and trying to define for herself who she wants to be outside of her mom's opinion of who she should be.

How did you work on the mother/daughter relationship with Hailee Steinfeld?
She's an absolute sweetheart. She's so bright and so open that it was easy enough to do. But with the pandemic guidelines, it was not as easy as it usually is. I saw half her face in rehearsal—and up until the moment we literally had to shoot on camera. We couldn't touch each other in the way that we normally can. So, honestly, the first time I had to hug her in the scene, it felt unusual... We just had to jump in and do it.

What do you like about Jeremy Renner as Hawkeye?
We have so many same interests outside of the realm of work, and we connect on so many different levels. So, honestly, it was nothing but frustrating for me that I didn't get more [scenes with him]! It's not fair calling this "work." This is play when it comes to actors like Jeremy Renner and Vincent D'Onofrio! ◉

01

01 Vera Farmiga as Eleanor Bishop, whose wealth hides some dangerous secrets.

BRIAN D'ARCY JAMES
DEREK BISHOP

Missing from the lives of his wife and daughter, Derek Bishop still has some
surprises in store for his family. Actor Brian d'Arcy James discusses the
complexity of the Bishops' familial relationships.

How did you approach playing Derek Bishop? I had to do my research and put my little sleuthing hat on to figure out what function he served, and how he fit in to the whole lexicon of this world. Ultimately, I was tasked with doing what the script requires. His role in this story is to represent the familial connection that he has with his daughter and the complexity of their familial relationship. So that's something that I really enjoyed and can relate to. I'm a father myself, so that was immediate for me.

He is a very grounded relevant character.
It's extreme because he's a person that has come from immense wealth and has been privileged from day one, even *before* day one. He just became a part of this lineage of wealth and power. That's also a very fitting storyline for today in terms of what we're dealing with, our eyes being awakened to what is privilege and why people get to think that they can behave the way they do. Derek has always operated in a bubble where he could get away with bending the rules or even breaking the rules. It's very interesting to be able to try to represent that and the less endearing qualities about this guy, in contrast with the very basic universal love that a father has for his daughter and his wife. ◉

01 Although morally ambiguous, Derek Bishop has a deep affection for his daughter, Kate.

TRACKSUIT MAFIA

The Tracksuit Mafia is the crazy tracksuit-clad crime organization that wreaks havoc across New York City. Aleks Paunovic, Carlos Navarro, and Piotr Adamczyk, who play senior mafia members Ivan, Enrique, and Tomas, recall how they became real-life bros while working on the show.

Who are the Tracksuit Mafia?

Carlos Navarro: Well, the Tracksuit Mafia are the official stars of the show, to be honest. I think the Tracksuit Mafia are obviously insane.

Aleks Paunovic: It's the faction of all the gangs that are in New York. There are different colors of tracksuits in different areas of New York, and we're the three [leaders] of the tracksuit [gangs]. We cause a lot of trouble, and Hawkeye causes a lot of trouble for us.

Piotr Adamczyk: We are not guys you would like to meet in a dark alley, but we are also funny and not very bright.

AP: It's pulled from the comic book, which is really great. There's a massive fanbase for the Tracksuit Mafia.

CN: Yeah, we would see the Tracksuit Mafia in the comic book, and it's like, "bro this" and "bro that." And we said, "Man, we have not been saying enough "bro's.'" So we were "bro"-ing it out. It was an honor to take on villains that people were looking forward to seeing in the Marvel Cinematic Universe.

The Tracksuit Mafia seem to enjoy making fun of Hawkeye…

CN: Yeah, I think this is the first time in MCU history where you have the villains straight-up making fun of a Super Hero to their face. There are several times where we're busting his balls.

AP: It's great because they don't really take themselves seriously, which made it so much fun for us.

Let's talk about those tracksuits…

PA: I had big expectations when I got the first text from ▶

01 The gang's all here! Behind-the-scenes on Marvel Studios' *Hawkeye*.

"We were really blessed that we all like each other. We just connected."

▶ Costumes [saying], "We have an exceptional costume for you..." The costume guy had to do this costume thousands and thousands of times.

AP: The tracksuit's great, but I [also] had alligator shoes.

PA: That means he's the boss.

AP: When they showed me those shoes, I was like, "I am in love with these."

CN: I got broke-down Vans.

Did you get time to build chemistry?

CN: Man, we were real lucky. We had about a month where we weren't shooting that much and we just spent a lot of time together. It really did build a lot of chemistry. These are my bros. I know it sounds cheesy, but I love these guys. We talk all the time.

AP: We have a Tracksuit Mafia text thread, and we always keep in contact.

PA: I'm Polish, and I have to thank you guys because, being a foreigner, sometimes it was difficult to understand what was going on on set with the film language slang. You guys helped me a lot, explaining what needed to be explained.

AP: Bro.

CN: Bro, man.

PA: But, you know, this bond helped us.

AP: Oh, yeah, when we were in New York we really felt it. We were really blessed that we all like each other. We just connected. We talked about the show. We talked about the different things that we would do or what we could bring, and helped each other on set too...

PA: Giving tips, improvising...

CN: Not all the time do you get to a set and meet people who are willing to improvise with you. And that's what happened here. We hit the ground running and were ready to bring that chemistry to the screen.

AP: In the Molotov cocktail scene we just went off and improvised and carried the scene on for another three minutes. We kept on jamming, and it was freeing.

Your characters feel very real.

CN: We talked about how to not make it too crazy, to keep it in reality. We would ask each other questions – "Hey, do you think you would say this? Or how would we do that?"

AP: We shot a scene where there's a lot of physical activity: I roll in, Tomas puts the bag over Hawkeye's head, and Enrique hits him with the bat. And there was a flow to it because of the energy that we have. It just rolled off the page for us, which was great. We kept it grounded.

CN: We were working at it every day. Having people that you have chemistry with and that you trust helps a lot.

What was it like working with Fra Fee and Alaqua Cox?

AP: We bonded with Fra Free in Atlanta and New York. It was great, because he's an extreme talent. Just to have him be a part of the whole Tracksuit Mafia and us following his lead during the show was great.

CN: He's our tracksuit bro as well.

PA: And Alaqua is incredible. It was visible from the first table read. When she started to speak with sign language, you could see how powerful her eyes are, how powerful the thought comes through. We all knew it would be a great performance.

CN: It's incredible. Being new [to acting] and jumping into a project like this and crushing it is so impressive.

AP: It was a really intimidating position for her to be in, especially with everything that she had

going on. The team supported her, but watching her develop into Echo was pretty cool to watch. And with Fra, you can feel his quiet intensity. There's a resonance in his performance, which helped us because the less he does, the more we do, and the more powerful he is.

Did you like the Christmas setting in New York City?
AP: It was the coolest thing. We were there during the holidays, so the Christmas [lights] were all lit up. Then we got word that we were gonna be shooting at Rockefeller Center, and we were like, "This is bucket list stuff!"
PA: But [this was] during a very special period where The City That Never Sleeps was really empty during the pandemic. So it was strange.
AP: When we shot in Times Square, [the empty streets] allowed us to have this amazing shot of one of the most iconic places in the world. Even when we were driving in our vans down Madison Avenue, we were like, "I can't believe we're doing this at four o'clock in the morning!" We were running down the street with our guns. It's like, "That doesn't happen in New York."
CN: I was born in New York. And so to be back with these guys driving around Rockefeller Center was one of those moments where you go, "Wow, I can't believe I'm doing this." We never lost that energy, because we knew that energy was going to transfer over to the show. ☻

02 Tough guys Enrique, Ivan Banionis, Maya Lopez, Kazi Kazimierczak, and Tomas.

03 Confrontoimg "Ronin," in actuality Kate Bishop.

04 Enrique tries to intimidate Clint Barton.

05 The gang, commanded by Wilson Fisk, cause carnage on the streets.

ALAQUA COX

MAYA LOPEZ

In her very first acting role, Alaqua Cox plays Maya Lopez–the leader of the Tracksuit Mafia. Cox recalls how she first found out about the role and talks about the impact the character has had on the deaf community.

How did you come to audition for the role of Maya Lopez?
First off, I'm from Wisconsin. I'm on the Menominee Native Reservation. I grew up there on the reservation my whole life. I never thought about being an actor until somebody sent me a link [to a casting site saying] they needed a female native, athletic, deaf person. And they're like, "This fits you! This is exactly who you are." And I looked at it, and I thought, "No, it's alright." Then another friend sent me the same link. And then a third friend sent me the link. So I thought, "Fine, I'll go ahead and apply." I emailed them, and they replied pretty quickly. Then we had correspondence, and they just wanted to know about me in a video. Then I had my first audition. I sent a video to them, and the rest of it's history.

What impact do you think the role has had on the deaf community?
Really, it's amazing that they actually cast a deaf person for a deaf character. It means that they're taking the right step in the right direction. I'm really happy because this is gonna have such an impact on the deaf community at large. It's definitely a big deal. I'm so excited about [the TV series] Echo.

To begin with, you didn't know you'd be playing a new MCU character who would be getting her own spin-off show…
Right, I had no idea this was gonna happen. They told me, and I was so shocked. I was like, "No, no, no, this is not real! You're getting your own show!" I had to ask them why. They're like, "Well, you've improved so much. People are so fascinated with what you've been

doing, and they're giving you your own show." They had so much confidence and trust in me.

Did you have to learn many stunts for the role?
My fighting style is mostly elbow strikes and hits. I was planning on punching, but they wanted to protect my hands. So they switched it to a lot of elbow work because I sign to communicate and they wanted to make sure that that was taken care of. My fighting style is more of an MMA style and karate - kinda some badass moves! But my stunt double did a lot of the kicks. There's certain angles where I couldn't move my prosthetic leg, and my stunt double did an amazing job with that.

I worked a lot on rehearsing stunts in the beginning with Heidi and Renae [Moneymaker, stunt coordinators]. They made me feel so comfortable and made sure that I didn't hurt myself doing a roundhouse kick. They were very motherly.

How would you describe Maya's relationship with Kazi?
Our relationship is very complicated. We have a love/hate relationship. We're were trying to hold our relationship away from the Tracksuit Mafia because we don't want to show [them] that romantic element. Then later, when you kind of find out that he's part of the plan to kill my father, there's that hate element that comes into it. It's a very rocky relationship.

How did you find the working with Fra Fee?
What's so great with Fra is that we rehearsed so much together and got to know each other outside of our characters. He's such a nice, sweet guy. He was so easy to ▶

02

03

> "I really love the costume from the final episode. It's my favorite throughout the whole *Hawkeye* show."

▶ work with because he studied sign language to make sure he was doing it perfectly, and he looks great on the screen, which I truly appreciate.

You also spent several days filming with Jeremy Renner, didn't you?
I worked with Jeremy on set probably for four days, but those four days were such an amazing experience, just watching him act. He's such an amazing actor. He knows how to shift those emotions so quickly. I learned so much just by watching him.

How did you find filming the big car chase?
It was so fun. It took three days for us to shoot the car chase scene. It was pretty funny because I saw the two guys in front of me making the car move, which was interesting to see while I was acting.

Are there advantages to being so new to acting?
Well, yes and no. Honestly, I was very nervous because I didn't know what I was doing as far as acting goes. It was such a new world to me. So coming in was definitely daunting. There was a lot of information that always came towards me, and sometimes I wanted that information filtered out. But I learnt new things every day.

How did you find working with directors Bert & Bertie?
I have to say I love Bert & Bertie. They always made sure that I was comfortable and that I didn't feel overwhelmed. This was the first time I'd acted, and it [involved] so much information, so many changes. They would always be supportive. They would say, "Take your time." And I was so appreciative. I only worked with Rhys [Thomas] one or two times, and he's definitely ▶

01 Maya Lopez as played by newcomer Alaqua Cox.

02 Maya hits the streets.

03 Lopez confronts the Kingpin.

04

04 Maya Lopez rides
into action on the
streets of New York.

05 A behind the
scenes moment as
Cox films an intense
action sequence.

06 Filming the
stunt-packed
car chase.

07 Maya Lopez's story
continues in Marvel
Studios' *Echo*.

05

▶ a nice gentleman. But mostly I worked with Bert & Bertie, and they definitely are very motherly.

What did you think of the costume in the final episode?
I really love the costume. It's my favorite throughout the whole *Hawkeye* show. I show who my character is. I show my prosthetic leg. A lot of people were surprised that she has a prosthetic. I'm so glad that they incorporated that because that's who I am. And I love the red leather pants. It just kind of makes me look very badass!

Your cousin was in the show, wasn't she?
Yeah, my little cousin Darnell [Besaw, who plays young Maya in the episode 'Echoes']. She's seven. There were three of us that were native, and that's so rare. I remember when I got the role and we were celebrating. "Oh, my God, I can't believe I'm in the Marvel world!" And my aunt was more worried about Darnell at first because she's such a shy little girl. But she did such an amazing job. I feel so grateful for this opportunity that they've given to all of us.

What has this experience meant to you?
On the last day, I just felt sad. After hugging people and saying goodbye, [I felt] so happy and excited, so many mixed emotions. But this opportunity means so much to me. I've met so many amazing and wonderful people, and it's been such an amazing experience. ☻

07

06

VINCENT D'ONOFRIO
KINGPIN

A familiar face to Daredevil fans, Vincent D'Onofrio's surprise reappearance as crime lord supreme Wilson Fisk, aka the Kingpin, heralded a welcome return for the character. Here, he discusses re-imagining his iconic role for the Marvel Cinematic Universe...

What attracted you to come back as Kingpin?
I got a call from my agent saying that Kevin Feige wanted to talk to me. So he called me, we talked, and he said he wanted to bring me into the MCU.. It was like, "Wow, okay. I'm not going to say no to that. That's pretty awesome."

I really loved playing this character. I liked creating him from the [comic book] art of guys like David Mack and Bill Sienkiewicz. The writers on the Netflix series were amazing too. So to go further in the canon of this character is just amazing. There's a complete change in the character, and it's so much fun.

What kind of process did you use to find the character again?
Trinh [Tran, executive producer], and I had talks, and I was able to explain how I feel about the character and what motivates [him]. So she was able to pass that onto the writers and to other people involved.

Once I got the scripts and read them, then I was able to dive in deeper with them. I sent them the art that I thought portrayed the character in this new world, because we already knew what he looked like back in the day. There were particular paintings—my favorite paintings from my favorite artists who I previously mentioned.

[The team] were so collaborative and wonderful. They just brought in different ideas, better ideas—they went with my ideas—it was like a great combination of all this stuff. We nailed it down to two particular photos that we actually kind of recreated from two different runs that involve Fisk. We also changed dialogue here and there according to the emotional aspect of the character, because Fisk is really driven by emotion. He's like a child and a monster both at the same time. So it got very intense.

Was it fun to explore the character at his worst?
After the Battle of New York he lost a lot of his connections and a lot of his money. He's in a desperate situation, but he's trying to gather up his power again and it's a struggle to maintain his dignity. There's this combination of him being down and out, and also trying to grasp his dignity and hold onto it. There's also the idea of him reminding his peers and everybody else around him that he is the boss. He is the mastermind. So, that's the gist of the character now. We're going to go further, but right now, that's who he is and we can grow from there. It's a new beginning for me as the actor playing him.

How did you come up with his new look?
That was taken from those photos I was talking about. On my laptop, the screensaver is a photo of Kingpin wearing the clothes—a Hawaiian shirt and the white suit (blazer and white pants)—from the comic *Family Business*. That's been on my screensaver for four years, and [during filming] I wore that exact suit.

Is it good to know where this character can go?
I think it's amazing. We've already started talking about the history between Maya and Kingpin and this very complicated relationship between the two of them —almost a father/daughter thing. There's a real history in the different runs of the relationship between Maya and Fisk. It gets very intense. There are a couple of great [comic] volumes between the two of them, [and there's] also some great art in those books. But it's a big deal, [and] it's a big deal to put them together in the same realm. There's a hint of how he feels about Maya in Marvel Studios' *Hawkeye*, and, Marvel Studios' *Echo* will take that even further. ◉

01 Vincent D'Onofrio
returns as Wilson
Fisk, the Kingpin.

FRA FEE

KAZI KAZIMIERCZAK

Self-confessed Marvel Cinematic Universe super-fan Fra Fee on
his time with the Tracksuit Gang and working with Alaqua Cox.

How did you feel about joining the MCU?
I was trying to play it as cool as possible. I had my meeting with the director, Rhys Thomas. I didn't let them know that I was an obscene fan of the MCU. I tried to play it very cool and very professional. But when I got the gig, I let them know that this is what dreams are made of!

Did you do much research?
I re-watched all the movies, keeping an eye on what Jeremy was doing. He had this real sense of human connection and empathy. Then I read a few of the Hawkeye comic books to get to know the characters more. My character was featured in the comic books, but they really redefined who Kazi is. I was able to put my own stamp on it. It was a lovely process getting to figure out who this person is.

Did you enjoy portraying Kazi's simmering rage?
When you can trust your camera operator, you have license to just be really small. That's a real thrill. There is a real quiet intensity to Kazi that I was figuring out while I was exploring his journey. There's a very fine line that he treads throughout, desperately wanting to work his way up the ranks, but being unable to do so because of Maya's position.

How did you find working with Alaqua Cox?
At the beginning of the process, I started learning sign language, initially to help me communicate with Alaqua on set and when we were rehearsing. The good thing is we had a lot of time to rehearse. That's not a normal thing in any film set, even on something of this size.

Alaqua is an extraordinary find. She has the ability to do so little and yet tell a million stories in her performance. And there's such an extraordinary vulnerability to her. I'm super excited for Echo's story to be told in the future.

Much of the communication between Kazi and Maya is through sign language.
There is something very interesting about acting without much voice. Sometimes I was SimComing, as it's referred to when you sign and voice at the same time. But for the little intimate moments with Maya, at most I was just whispering. It was so quiet. All you could hear was the breeze in the cemetery or the cars outside. It was an incredible way to perform. We were reading off each other. I was brought into her quiet world, which is actually extremely expressive.

Was it tough to do the blue and green screen work?
When you're reading things like "this arrow blows up to 50 times its size and comes crashing down like a tree trunk," you have to use your imagination. But at the same time you're also using your Marvel imagination. You can picture how they're going to turn that into reality on screen. Whenever you're asked to use your imagination as an actor, it's a real thrill.

How did you feel about Kingpin's return?
In the early versions of this script, the boss man was known as "Oxygen Mask Man." Later, Trinh [Tran, executive producer] pulled me aside and said, "OK, we've got our boss man. It's Kingpin, and he's going to be played by Vincent D'Onofrio." I was like, "What? Are you kidding me?" Of all of the villains I can think of, Kingpin is the most iconic. And so to have Vincent there in the iconic white suit is awesome. The feeling on set was like everything else about this experience, it was a lovely family vibe. ◉

01 Fra Fee as the
would be leader of
the Tracksuit Mafia,
Kazi Kazimierczak.

01 Lila joins her dad and her brothers, Nathanial and Cooper, to attend a performance of *Rogers: The Musical.*

AVA RUSSO

LILA BARTON

Lila Barton is the daughter of Clint Barton, who wants nothing more than for her father to come home for Christmas. Ava Russo tells us why she was excited to return to the role she previously played in Marvel Studios' *Avengers: Endgame.*

How did you feel when you heard you were going to reprise the character of Lila in Hawkeye?
It was super awesome. My dad [Marvel Studios' *Avengers: Infinity War* and Marvel Studios' *Avengers: Endgame* co-director Joe Russo] came into the room and was like, "Ava, I've got some exciting news." He told me, and I was just ecstatic because it was one of my first big roles. To be able to continue and be able to get more into Lila felt really good. Being able to give her a backstory like that is very cool.

How does Lila feel about Clint retiring as Hawkeye at the end of the show?
I feel like maybe [his family] don't really believe that it's going to happen in all honesty. Because he's been saying it for years. "Oh, I'm going to retire. We're going to be a family again. We're going to be able to spend some time together and actually bond." And then he keeps getting dragged back in. I feel like Lila, as a character, has sort of given up hope.

How fun was it to watch *Rogers: The Musical* in the show?
It's was so cool and really well done. It looked like a real professional Broadway show. Being able to be behind the scenes and watch it unfold was just so sick and so awesome! ◉

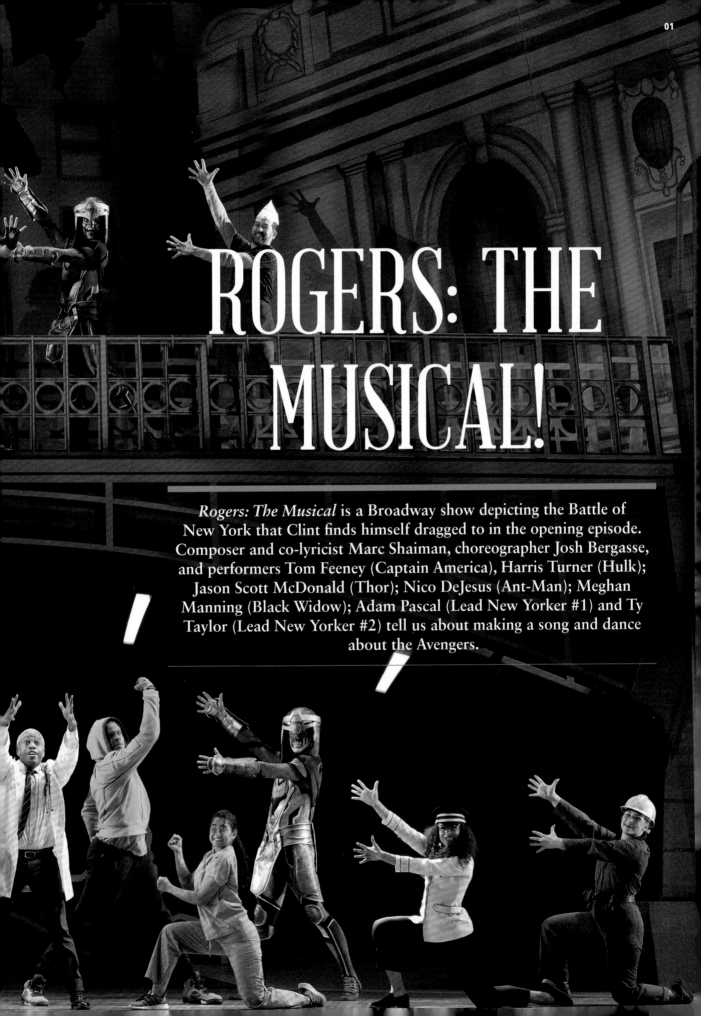

ROGERS: THE MUSICAL!

Rogers: The Musical is a Broadway show depicting the Battle of New York that Clint finds himself dragged to in the opening episode. Composer and co-lyricist Marc Shaiman, choreographer Josh Bergasse, and performers Tom Feeney (Captain America), Harris Turner (Hulk); Jason Scott McDonald (Thor); Nico DeJesus (Ant-Man); Meghan Manning (Black Widow); Adam Pascal (Lead New Yorker #1) and Ty Taylor (Lead New Yorker #2) tell us about making a song and dance about the Avengers.

"Through the script, it was clear that Hawkeye doesn't really like the way he is presented on stage."

Marc, how did you go about writing the song "Save the City?"

Marc Shaiman: Deep down, no matter what the medium you're writing for, you pretty much start with the same foundation, which is figuring out what is the story the song is telling? What is the feeling and the emotion? That's where my co-lyricist, Scott Wittman, is so good. He's the one who said, "Shouldn't it be the New Yorkers saying, 'Save the city; help us, Avengers!'?" That's sort of all I needed to hear. Then I wrote a dummy version of the song and we finessed it.

Marvel Studios sent me the script of the Battle of New York from the *Avengers* movie. And we were just grabbing all the great lines. Like "Tesseract" and "Chitari" and "Let's get some shawarma." I mean, there were all these things that stuck out. And [we] figured out, "Can we think of a rhyme for that or not?"

What tone did you want for the musical?

Josh Bergasse: The big question when I first was brought on to this was, what is the tone? Is it a hit? It a comedy? Is it serious? And, you know, they said it's a hit. It's serious, but inherently the idea of an Avengers musical is funny. And the song is awesome. It's got some really funny moments to it. So I wanted to make it a really cool production number where you see great production values, great dancing, great singing. But then I wanted to give some really funny moments, especially for the Marvel fans and people who know the movie and know the Battle of New York.

Marc Shaiman: When we were writing the song we knew that it had to be a full-force Broadway musical number, but we also knew that it had to, in some ways, be something that would make Hawkeye's eyes roll, because he was in the

real life version of this [battle]. To see it put into Broadway musical terms is, for him, probably a little like, "I cannot believe this!" There's always a great smart-alecky kind of humor that runs through all the Marvel Studios films. So we tried to balance all that. I think when you watch the number you laugh at it a little, but it's also a rousing song.

Josh Bergasse: We were trying to make sure that it was worthy of a giant Broadway production number.

Marc Shaiman: Josh has a great muscular kind of feel to his choreography, which perfectly matches the Avengers and the Marvel Cinematic Universe.

How did you want to portray Hawkeye in the musical?

Marc Shaiman: Through the script, it was clear that Hawkeye doesn't really like the way he is presented on stage. He's constantly kind of being interrupted or upstaged, and that was something they really finessed in the staging of how Captain America's shield goes in front of Hawkeye's face. [Clint] doesn't really like the idea that there's a musical. He thinks, "Couldn't I have been treated a little better?"

Josh Bergasse: For the episode, we needed Clint to have the reaction to Hawkeye being kind of misrepresented in the musical. But we wanted to make sure that the

01 The cast of *Rogers: The Musical* take to the stage!

02 Executive producer Trinh Tran surveys the set.

03 The cast and crew assemble to pose for a group photo.

writers of *Rogers: The Musical* wouldn't purposely make Hawkeye the joke. So it was tricky. How do you stay true to the show-within-the-show but still make sure that you're serving the purpose of the arc in the episode? We tried a bunch of different ways of achieving that. You could do so much in the editing room. You could do so much with reactions and things like that.

How fun was it to see the song come to life on stage?
Josh Bergasse: It had been a rough year. The pandemic had been particularly hard on the live performing arts and dance. So, for a lot of the performers, in rehearsal for this, I think that was the first moment of, "Oh, gosh, we're back. We're doing it again."
Adam Pascal: It felt so great to finally get it on stage and in front of people. I was back on stage doing what I do for a living.
Harris Turner: The first day we walked into the fabulous Fox, I just like took a breath and said a silent prayer. It was like, "It feels good to be home."
Tom Feeney: I knew a lot of the people in this cast, and it was an absolute blast to get back in the room with everyone. We threw everything and the kitchen sink into this. It was exhausting, but so much fun.

Jason Scott McDonald: Getting to play Thor was something I'd never thought I would actually get to do. And then the transformation of a new beard and a wig, the actual hammer...
Nico DeJesus: It was really cool to know that they were gonna include Ant-Man in this historic battle!
Marc Shaiman: To see this huge cast singing lyrics that you wrote down in your basement at the piano, it's always freaky to me. Music just flows out of me, but writing lyrics is what I really love to do. And so me and Scott, when we write lyrics, that's the thing I cherish the most. It's so weird to [see] other humans say these words that you wrote... but they make it come alive. Without them it's nothing.

What did you think of the set?
Josh Bergasse: The design of it was really cool. It kind of looked like it popped out of a comic book. A lot of the stuff felt very two-dimensional with the forced perspective and everything!

Was the process much different than working on a real Broadway show?
Josh Bergasse: If I were doing this number for Broadway, ▶

▶ I'd have to be a little more specific with making sure that the audience knows where to look in order to follow the story and follow the characters, because this is a big number on a big set. If you lose the audience, if they don't know where to follow everything, they'll get lost. Whereas, when we do it for film, we rely a little bit more on the camera to do that... But you want to make sure you have beautiful dancing and beautiful backgrounds and exciting things happening in the shot as well. So you have to make sure that you have things happening in the shot that aren't just about watching one lead, so the audience understands, "Oh, there's all this other stuff happening on stage" and they have that feeling that they're watching a big Broadway production number.

Adam Pascal: I was surprised at how similar it is to what I actually do for a living when I do a show on Broadway. The difference is that you normally have four weeks to learn an entire show. And the entire show is built sort of piece by piece, and you work on scenes, you work on music. When we came into this whole thing, it was kind of already built and we immediately started learning choreography. By the second day we kinda learned the whole number.

Ty Taylor: I hadn't done a Broadway show in about 25 years. I was thinking that it was gonna be easy. I thought it was gonna be a musical that felt like a TV show and [we] weren't going to have to do much choreography and I wasn't gonna be sweating for eight hours a day in a rehearsal. As it turned out, we were doing a real musical!

How did you approach the show's stunts?

Meghan Manning: I'm a technical dancer, but I have always loved to do tricks. I've been working on kip-ups and special tricks my whole life. [For this] I trained a little bit in stunt work and didn't really know how it would come together. But this job was such a fun one because it put together my dance and my stunt training.

Josh Bergasse: The cool thing was a lot of the dancers had these special skills where they did a back flip or a kip up. Or they could do these great jumps or they do aerial work where they're comfortable flying. Then the Marvel Studios stunt coordinator, Heidi [Moneymaker], came in, and she could do everything they could do. She was like, "Oh, you mean this?" And she did that. Then she went to somebody else, "Oh, you mean this?" And she did that. So she could do everything... The day she came into rehearsal was really cool. I asked her to come in and look at what we're doing and just make it look a little cooler.

How exciting was is that they showed the full musical number in the final episode?

Josh Bergasse: I can't even put it into words. Normally when I come onto a show like this, they just want a little snippet. If they want 30 seconds or 20 seconds, they'll have me choreograph a minute or two minutes and they're not very excited about it. But the support for this production

04

04 "Loki" busts some moves as the theatrical invasion of the Chitauri begins!

05 A castmember has their Chitauri makeup applied.

was incredible. The excitement from everybody, top down, was so cool.

What I like to do is tell a story through dance and musicals. So sometimes if I'm doing an abridged thing, it's not as fulfilling because it's kind of background. But the fact that they wanted to commit to doing the full number was just so cool... This was a huge highlight in my career.

Could this be a real Broadway musical?

Adam Pascal: I think it could. And I think it will. That's my personal opinion! When a show is successful, there's a lot of money to be made. And Disney knows how to produce musicals. So I would not be surprised if this was the seed to create some sort of Marvel Super Hero type musical.

Jason Scott McDonald: I hope this expands the world of Marvel creations and we get a musical world. I think it would be a lot of fun.

Meghan Manning: I could totally see this show on Broadway. There could be so many special effects, but also that dance goes so hand-in-hand with action. I think all the Marvel fans would love it.

Josh Bergasse: I'd love that. Listen, I was a huge Marvel comic collector, and Avengers was one of my main comics that I collected. So, for me doing Broadway on TV and it being the Avengers is so cool. ◉

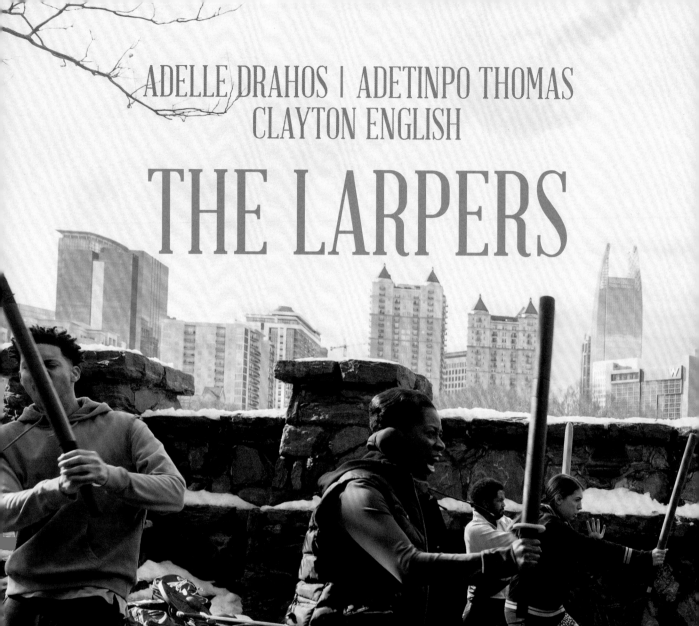

ADELLE DRAHOS | ADETINPO THOMAS
CLAYTON ENGLISH

THE LARPERS

01

When Clint goes to retrieve his Ronin suit, he comes face to face with the LARPers (or live action role-players)—a group who wear elaborate costumes, take on historical roles, and re-enact huge mock-battles with foam weapons. Three actors who play key LARPers—Clayton English (Grills), Adelle Drahos (Missy), and Adetinpo Thomas (Wendy)—look back on dressing up, helping the heroes, and pulling heroic poses.

"This is a crowd that loves the Super Hero world... We're here to help be a representation for the fanbase of these shows."

What do you like about the LARPers?
Adetinpo Thomas: We bring a lot of levity. I think we also are moral support in a lot of ways too. Clint and Kate end up leaning on us... We're fun and we're funny and we're there to be friends and to help out.

Adelle Drahos: I love just the whole idea of the LARPers because these are people who really love the fantasy fiction world, who really dive deep into it, who get a lot of fulfillment out of it. This is also your same crowd that tends to be into the comic book world as well. I won't say all comic book people are into LARPing, but I would say there's probably a good amount of LARPers who are into comic books because they do like fantasy fiction.

Clayton English: They're fully dressed [with] foam swords, big battle sequences, all that type of stuff. In the series, Grills does it with a few other friends of his, and they're all first responders. It's almost their way of like letting out their frustration. It's a little like a nerdier bowling league. Don't come at me, because it's not nerdy. It's great!

Adelle Drahos: This is a crowd that loves the Super Hero world... We're here to help be a representation for the fanbase of these shows.

How important are your characters to the story?
Clayton English: Since [Grills is] a firefighter, I can kinda patch up people when they need it. Two people work for the police department, [and] they have access to files, they have access to the evidence room. We're pretty eager to help. Who doesn't want to help an Avenger? They done saved the world a few times over now.

Adelle Drahos: Missy designs the LARPer costumes for the group. She loves to get her hands dirty, to stitch-and-needle and build the outfits, which is really fun because I've always loved playing dress up myself. I still do. That's one reason why I like acting! She gets her inspiration from the historical aspect of it as well as fantasy fiction. You're allowed to be creative in your designs and take your own liberties because as a LARPer you get to create this world. It's all at the will of your imagination, so she kinda likes to do a little bit of a mix of both. Then when pulling in the super suits, you get to insert some functionality as well. Like, "This could actually be hit with an arrow or a bullet. Let's try to put on something that could deflect that" - versus lightweight foam, which is generally what you would use in a LARP, because there's no need to be sweating more than you need to be.

01 The LARPers (live-action role players) in action!

02 Kate Bishop acquaints herself with the LARPers led by Wendy Conrad.

03 The team flank Executive Producer Trinh Tran (center).

Adetinpo Thomas: My character is based on one of the comic book characters, Wendy Conrad. Her alias is Bombshell... I'm often the voice of reason, getting the group to rally together. I'm often kind of giving this look like, "Y'all, Clint needs us!"

How familiar were you with the MCU?

Clayton English: Man, I am all the way in. I'm a big Marvel fan. Like me and my brother, that was our thing - coming up from the comic books to the cartoons to when the Marvel movies started and just going to see those. To be a part of it is huge for me because I'm a super fan. I really like the storyline. I read the Hawkeye [comic] series that this is kind of based off of, so when I got there it was like, "I'm fanning out. I'm seeing Jeremy Renner. I'm seeing Hailee. I'm seeing Pizza Dog." It was great.

Adelle Drahos: I never read the comics, but I have always loved the movies. I really love the world, the plot devices, the Super Hero shtick.

Adetinpo Thomas: I am not so obsessed that I've read every comic. But when Endgame came out, I re-watched the entire series in chronological order... Walking on, everyone was wearing Avengers swag from the last show they worked on. That's exciting.

What was it like working with Jeremy Renner?

Clayton English: Jeremy just got so much knowledge about what he's doing, and he shares that with you. That was kinda cool. Like, he would explain what shots were going [on] and what we had coming up, and [suggest], "OK, maybe you should be here." Those types of things helped ground me a little bit, because for the first couple days I was like, "Oh, that's Hawkeye!"

Adelle Drahos: It was fun to see [Jeremy] riff. What's nice is that, while we stuck to the script, there was some improv involved. You really got to play with the character. And with him riffing, I was able to riff a little bit with that. As someone with an improv background, that was fun.

Clayton English: His adlibs are hilarious. He threw me for a loop a few times, just saying stuff that was off-the-cuff.

What did you think of your costumes?

Clayton English: To see it go from on paper to actually getting made it was super cool. I hope I get to use it again. It's got cool shoulder pads, leather. It gave me a Doctor Strange feel, but it was also a little Asgardian.

Adelle Drahos: Mine has a full chainmail dress, which is heavy. It probably added around a good 15 or 20 extra pounds. Then I have these shoulder pads... So it took a moment to get used to moving in the suit. Once you broke into it, it was a little empowering. I'm not gonna lie. You felt cool... It has this knight/Viking/Super Hero vibe to it, which is all of the things I've ever wanted to play. I feel very honored. ⬤

ADAM LYTLE
HEIDI MONEYMAKER
NOON ORSATI
STUNTS

Adam Lytle (Fight Coordinator), Heidi Moneymaker (Stunt Coordinator) and Noon Orsati (Second Unit Stunt Coordinator) are part of the team who made sure that Clint Barton and Kate Bishop are put through their paces in Marvel Studios' *Hawkeye*.

How did you go about devising the fighting styles for the characters?
Heidi Moneymaker: This was a bit of a challenge in the sense that we had so many characters, and I really wanted them to all have their own flair and own style. Sometimes you come in and there's already a depicted style or characters who fight similarly and whatnot. But for this there were reasons to have them all be different.

Clint Barton has a somewhat established style. But he comes into this show as a retired Super Hero living with his family. He has hearing loss and is wearing a hearing aid. His back hurts. He's kind of the John Wick of the Marvel Studios series, minus all the murder. For me, I always thought of him like that - let's keep his style and the flair, what he's always done, but think a little bit in the John Wick sense of everything always hurts. "I'm getting too old for this. I'm still winning, but it's a lot more of a struggle now."

▶

01 Jeremy Renner and Hailee Steinfeld in a behind the scenes action shot.

02 Clint and Kate take on the Tracksuit Mafia.

03 Clint and the LARPers in battle.

04 Expert swordsman Jack Duquesne shows off his skills.

05 Jeremy Renner rehearses an action sequence.

► We started with his fight style just coming in with what he's always done - archery and judo and straight boxing. We settled on a little more trapping and close quarters attacks because he was able to be very powerful in that sense. To me it reads a little more like, "OK, this is a smart tactic versus what a younger Super Hero might do, which is take more chances, do bigger swinging motions and bigger kicks and flare out." He just keeps someone close and takes them down. And, of course, he's still amazing with his bow and arrow, so there's a lot of archery in there as well. But it was important to depict his newfound style and what he had to do to be smart.

Then we moved into Kate Bishop. We wanted her to be very similar to him because she's idolized him her whole life. But she's a woman and she's had some different training. So we have her doing a little Judo, but mostly Aikido. We had her do things that you would buy that a trained female could do, so there's not a lot of big, swinging punches and things that a guy would do against a guy. The [moves] are very feminine but still strong, also using her brain and using found objects and being really quick-witted.

In the wine cellar fight, she ends up there in this Ronin [suit]. All of a sudden things are blowing up and going crazy. This is kind of her first time fighting and figuring out like, "Oh, this is not like it is in the gym or in training. This is real." So we have her picking up wine bottles and knocking things over and just being smart and scrappy and getting her way through this whole fight.

Her character does very much evolve as she's working with Clint Barton and seeing how he moves and how he works. She does tries a couple of his moves and fails but ultimately makes them better towards the end, so we have a little buildup there. Ultimately he recognizes that she's actually very good and very fast learning, quick witted, and he starts working together with her as a team. That was a big story point for us.

How much is Clint Barton's fighting style rooted in his character?

Adam Lytle: One of the things we wanted to nail was each character's style. Clint Barton was one of the early ones where we were like, "OK, he was an Avenger. He went rogue for a while, became the Ronin and developed his style further. But now he just wants to live a normal life." We wanted to bring that into the role. This is a guy with immense skills, a very capable person. But he doesn't want to do it anymore, and his character reflects that.

A lot of what we wanted to do with him was very close quarters, tactical stuff, using the environment to his

advantage. He's thinking as a tactician, rather than, "How can I use my powers here?" I mean, his weapon [a bow and arrows] is a perfect example of that as well. So using that mindset where he will get in close and use every part of his body as a weapon rather than relying on super speed or super strength. He uses his mind, and that's the most important thing he has.

It was great when we were first training him in prep. I remember him coming in, and his input was amazing. He had his own ideas of what the character should be, and that is invaluable for people that are creating action, because you want a character that's truthful and not just a bunch of meaningless moves.

That was a great opportunity for us to pick his brain and see how he saw Clint Barton now he has turned over a new leaf. And he killed it, man... He was fast, and he goes hard. Once he gets it, you're going in for a ride. If he's throwing you, you'd better prepare to hit the ground! I loved his enthusiasm, and he picks up stuff so fast.

What was your take on Maya and the Tracksuit Mafia?
Heidi Moneymaker: With the Maya character, that's a whole new ballgame because now you're looking at, "OK, she's deaf and she's missing part of one of her limbs. What's her power source? Let's go back to where ▶

"I didn't want [Maya] to punch with her hands because that's how she communicates..."

she's coming from. She's full of anger and hate, and she wants to avenge her father's death. So what does she do? She trains her whole life."

One of the things for me is I didn't want her to punch with her hands. I didn't want her to damage her hands because that's how she communicates, so everything she did was solid with knees, elbows, big kicks with her big metal leg, throwing people through walls. But it was important for me to have that kind of thought process of why would she damage the one thing that helps her communicate in the world? That was sort of our premise for Maya and what we did with her. And [we] really used this limb of hers – titanium, I believe - and showed it as a power source instead of a disability.

Then we had Kazi and the Tracksuits. They're thugs. They're gangsters. Everything they do is just straight up punching. They have metal pipes, weapons - think Sopranos but Russian and with less death! So they kinda have their own gangster style, but I wanted Kazi to stand out because he's supposed to be the leader of this group. When Fra [Fee] came in and we started training with him, we really worked with him on a personal level. To me the traditional sense of training didn't flow with how his body moved. He moved way differently, and so we did like a Brad Pitt *Snatch* kind of wildcat chaos character for him. It really worked out well. He hunched his shoulders a little when he moved, so he used it as a tactic. And we had him doing all these crazy things that were confusing to opponents. And when he struck and when he punched, it was a hard hit and you didn't know where it was coming from. A lot of people get hit by this. That was our evolution with his fight style and character.

Then there's Yelena...

Heidi Moneymaker: That one was pretty easy because she's trained just like Natasha Romanoff and Black Widow. We just had to put a little bit of a different flair on it for her. We used some of the Black Widow moves I'd used in the past, but also used her move in Black Widow. She's a bit more scrappy than Natasha Romanoff, but still had been trained the same way. So it was a little bit of a throwback, but at the same time she gave it her own flair. It was nice when we finally got to work with Florence because she got to put her little spin on it.

Does stunt training always come naturally to you?
Heidi Moneymaker: Well, I will say I love that this role

is very physical. I've always been into training my body and engaging in physical activity. I love that this job left me no excuse but to get to a place where I would be shown something – whether it was right before a take or months in advance – and I would be able to pick up quickly. It didn't just happen, I had to prep for that.

It sounds as though Hailee Steinfeld was quick to learn the fight choreography too.
Adam Lytle: We have a long point in training so we can see what the actors are capable of and really develop their physical performance and their skill set. But right away Hailee jumped into this thing, and she was leaps and bounds ahead of a lot of people I've seen before.

She had a great body awareness. She listened and understood what we were saying when we were talking to her about physical notes and things like that. She picks up choreography extremely fast. It's such a blessing to be able to work with an actress that talented.

Noon, how did you design the driving stunts?
Noon Orsati: For us, the beats are prescribed in a sense. You have a conglomeration of people, the producers, the writers - and Kevin Feige, of course, who has come with an

idea of what he wants for this to shine. It's up to us to take this vision, incorporating our own vision and knowhow of how to accomplish it, to get it done.

Again, it takes a lot of people to make these action beats, especially something like the driving sequence, come to fulfillment in a safe and exciting way. It's the special effects guys, it's the transportation [team], it's the picture car guys that make the cars have the capability of doing the stunts. For the car sequence, we'd take it out to a large parking lot that would allow us to get up to the speeds that we wanted to shoot. Then we tried to make it all happen according to the pre-viz that we had. A lot of times the pre-viz would be in animatic form. They're basic cartoons that are presented to you. Now you have to add real life people, real life cars, real life scenarios to the animatic. And hopefully, everybody is happy that it looks close to the original conception. When that happens, you feel like you've won the world because you're making everybody happy and it looks great to the audience.

Did the fact that the car chase involved other stunts make it more challenging?
Noon Orsati: Yes, indeed. Again, the first thing in my mind was how to make it safe. We had to strap a girl to ▶

06 Kate Bishop battles the Kingpin.

07 The LARPers train in the park.

08 Kate Bishop in action on the ice.

09 Behind the scenes as Kate Bishop takes on the Tracksuit Mafia.

10 The carefully coordinated climactic battle goes before the camera.

"I thought it was better if the [fight] was a little more raw."

▶ a moving car that was in a joust sort of situation. It was going down a very narrow area. There were things on either side and/or moving cars coming either to or away from [the heroes] while she was hanging out the window shooting a bow and arrow either direction. For all intents and purposes, we did everything practically. But, we pulled from our intellect and from our experiences.

Can you talk about the biscuit rig?
Noon Orsati: The biscuit rig allows us to put the body of a car on top of another very low car that has a large engine. It's driven from up top or either side of the car on a pod, whatever is gonna suit best the shot. In this particular case, we had a 360-degree shot that had all sorts of action happening at the same time. The magic shot we wanted for the directors was that we would have the two actors playing this scene in the car while doing crazy driving, head-on near misses, side swipes, cars cutting in front, doors opening, people firing guns. Everything had to be meticulously planned. So we took our time. We went out and rehearsed this very well.

We didn't do that with the biscuit rig at first. We just went inside the car, did our first pass of what this 360-degree shot would look like. We stitched a few pieces together, so while it looks like it's done in one fluid 360-degree [movement], in reality we broke it up - through the VFX team - into different little aspects.

The biscuit allows a stunt driver to be driving the vehicle while the actors look like they're driving it. They're able to communicate. They're able to say their lines and play off of each other without the worry of, "Oh my God, I gotta miss this car to the left, now I gotta throw a 180!" All they have to think about their acting, the excitement of the scene. Jeremy and Hailee both had such a smile on their face at the end of the day. It looked like a lot of fun. Meanwhile, here in the stunt department, we were biting our nails! But everything worked just plum perfect. The stunt drivers that we brought in were great.

Heidi, did the emotional aspects of the story affect how you planned out the fight sequences??
Heidi Moneymaker: This might be one of the first times in my career with doing fight choreography that I was trying to pull [back on] the action a little bit. There was one time when I was talking to Rhys [Thomas, director] about pulling some of the action back because I thought it was better if it was a little more raw. ◉

MAYA SHIMOGUCHI

PRODUCTION
DESIGN

Marvel Studios' *Hawkeye* is filled with intricately designed
sets, including the Kingpin's restaurant, the 30 Rock bar and
the *Rogers: The Musical* backdrop. Production designer Maya
Shimoguchi reveals more about the process behind her craft.

Much of the series was shot on location in New York. How did that affect the production design?
We were in New York because we wanted to make sure we got all of the holiday stuff that normally happens. That was not something that we could've ever achieved here [in Atlanta]. [The Christmas atmosphere] is amazing and really filters through the entire city. There's [the Christmas celebration at] 30 Rock, which is a big extravaganza, and a big tree. But then there's all different types of Christmases that go on throughout the entire city and in Brooklyn and Queens that are funny and sometimes sad. They added so much to the story.

Did the pandemic make the process more manageable?
Yeah, and not just at 30 Rock, [but] the streets in general. There were people out but they weren't nearly as crowded. Like, we shot in Times Square. There were people there, but it wasn't the normal volume. So we did really benefit from the pandemic. And it kind of played into the Blip and the people returning and New York not being the same place that it once was.

What tone did you want the look of the show to have?
When we first started on it, I talked to the directors and we tried to find a way to inject a certain amount of color blocking into the sets so that it was more colorful than real

life, which I think is a good way of referencing back to the comic books.

Palette-wise, we were using colors to represent characters. Maya's palette was always in the yellows and greens. And Kate's palette was always in pink and purple because that ends up being sort of her color. We didn't adhere to it in a slavish way, but we kept on referring back to those mainstays.

As far as the 30 Rock bar, which was at the end of the whole thing, we were going into this black and gold color story that had to do with what's actually there at 30 Rock. We were tying that back to the [Kingpin]'s penthouse, which is also in a black and gold theme but in a weirder way because they both kind of represent the pinnacle of the characters' criminal enterprises. There were a lot of things where we tried to create continuity and also a better visual tone to hold things together.

01 Kate Bishop's place includes details such as targets and punch bags used for her training.

02 Behind the scenes as the crew film in the ice.

03 A specially rigged car used for filming.

04 Filming on the streets of New York.

You recreated aspects of 30 Rockefeller Plaza in Atlanta for some scenes. How difficult was that?
We modeled the entire 30 Rock Plaza, and we had some really excellent 3-D modelers. Doing that enabled us to really figure out the parts that we could build and what would make sense. You could preview what that was gonna look like and you could see where the set extension would be. It made it a lot more manageable.

A huge part for me was that we were able to go [to ▶

30 Rock] twice. We scouted it in October, and then we went back and did our shooting in December. So by the time we were into building the set [in Atlanta], we were really familiar with it and could hone in on the things that were necessary.

Can you explain the process of augmenting buildings?
When we built a set and you could see the skyline of Manhattan out of the windows, we'd have a blue screen. They digitally replaced that blue screen with footage that they shot of New York. Also, when we were shooting in Atlanta after a certain point they might "top" the buildings, make them taller. They added a layer of buildings behind that didn't exist.

They planned really well for how to achieve that. We're lucky in that there was a really amazing VFX team. They spent an extra two weeks in New York capturing footage of the city. So all of the extensions look great.

05

"[The set] was like LEGO—it could break apart and be reassembled."

Well, in the flashback he's in his mobster's penthouse, and this is supposed to represent that he's at the very height of his abilities. We looked at a [real] penthouse that was obviously very expensive. There were expensive things in it, but maybe it was done with some questionable taste choices. We were sticking with the black and gold theme to tie it into the 30 Rock bar. We had a lot of direction from Trinh [Tran, producer] about what the character is like, which helped us to understand which way to go with it.

As far as [Kingpin's] restaurant, they'd seen a restaurant that they liked in Atlanta, but it was impossible to shoot in. One day we were shooting in a cemetery and there was a greenhouse there. I looked at it and thought I could empty out this greenhouse and turn it into a version of the restaurant that they liked. And that's what we ended up doing! We went back to the cemetery, emptied out the greenhouse, and then put layers and layers of colored plex and corrugation and acrylics beads and created a very different atmosphere that is supposed to represent how far he's fallen.

Can you talk about the production design for *Rogers: The Musical*?

It was like a show inside of a show. It was super fun to create a set of that size. And then working with the material, the song, and the choreography, it became a very fun experience. You really felt the magic of the theatre. It was definitely my favorite day of shooting. In order to have one song for the musical we had to do a complete theatre set. The theatre that we used in Atlanta, the Fox Theatre, has a large stage, and we [also] did a scale model and concept illustrations.

[We made] pieces of New York City that were made in panels. There were these really specific physical sizes that no piece could go beyond because we had to get it into the theater! All of the flats [pieces of theatrical scenery] were made with fabric stretched on aluminum frames. They weren't solid and they were super lightweight so they could just like fly up into the air really quickly.

We had a physical bridge that was the front part of our set, which was built on another stage, also out of aluminum pieces. It was like LEGO – it could break apart and be reassembled... The bridge was really built as a bridge. It had a span, like 45 feet. Most of it was cutouts. We tried to stay true to it feeling like a gigantic pop-up book and also feeling like a comic book come to life. ◉

What did you want the Bishop mansion to say about Eleanor and Kate?

We see the Bishop mansion two times. We see it in the flashback when she's eight years old, and then we see it in present day. In the flashback we used a much warmer tone throughout the house. It was more playful. There's a warmer feeling, even in the furniture. Then in the present day, the temperature is much cooler, and there's a much more uptight, restricted, curated feel to the house, which is meant to represent her, obviously.

In the flashback [Kate is] having kind of an idealized childhood. Since we're seeing it more from memory, it makes it even more idealized because how you remember things is always nostalgic. That contrasts with how she perceives her mom to be controlling and strict, which we tried to represent in the [present day] house.

How did you make sure the Kingpin's sets represent his character?

05 A high rise set prior to being augmented to look much taller.

06 The Bishops' lavish dining room set.

MICHAEL CROW

COSTUME

Michael Crow has created costumes for Marvel Studios' *The Falcon and The Winter Soldier* and was assistant costume designer on several of the movies. He tells us how Marvel Studios' *Hawkeye* offered him an opportunity to put fresh spins on classic costumes and create some striking new designs.

What was your jumping off point for the costumes in the show?

When we started talking about the world of Hawkeye, we spent a lot of time looking at the Matt Fraction comics and the illustrations by David Aja. They created this strong visual world that was very bold and simple, and we really wanted to emulate that. So I tried to use a lot of texture but simple colors, not a lot of pattern, not a lot of fussy elements, trying to keep everything very rudimentary.

Did you draw upon Hawkeye's previous costumes?

I wanted to hearken back to some of the costumes that he's worn on the farm and at home but I also knew that we were going to carry some of those elements through to the fight scenes. So we built in elements of that costume. We stripped away the barn coat and the denim jacket and added hoodies and other elements that would allow us to get darker as the story went along. But we wanted him to start [with] a warm, textural tone to symbolize that he's trying to recapture that element of his life now that his family has returned.

How did you decide upon Kate's first look in the show?

We discussed Kate a lot, and it went in a lot of different directions. We didn't want her to be too fashiony. We felt like her wardrobe needed to feel very utilitarian. That said, she comes from a wealthy family. Her clothes don't need to be cheap. Her idea of buying a pair of jeans might be going to Bergdorf [Goodman, luxury department store], just because that's where she's used to going.

How did you approach Hawkeye's new costumes?

[Kate's] idea is that [Clint] needs something about his costume that stands out so he will appeal to people and be recognizable. But in keeping with the utility of everything, we wanted the costumes to feel a little bit more like sportswear. A lot of Super Hero costumes have a lot of bulk to them, or feel restrictive in certain ways. We wanted this to look like they look like they could move in them and really do the things that they need to do. They're practical costumes. We also gave [Clint] that iconic arrow chevron on his chest, again, hearkening to the Fraction run on the *Hawkeye* comic book.

Clint and Kate end up with matching Hawkeye outfits.

Yeah, it is the moment in the story where they become a team. This is the moment where you really want them to feel like they're connected. We brought the design elements like the chevron and the various shades of purple and black into the designs so that they feel like they work together well.

A lot of the chevrons or the "V's" in the costumes are representative of an arrow shape or the fletching on the arrows. We also added the element [from] the comic books that Kate has a cutout in her shoulder. And we added the shoulder armor on her costume and also a circular element on Jeremy's shoulder that relates to that design element from the comics.

If you look at Kate's pants, there's chevron elements on one of the legs and on the back of the calves. We used little pieces of fabric and elements to just pop the purples in different ways.

Did you use the Ronin costume from the previous films?

We had a few different versions of the Ronin costume. For the flashback with Clint killing William, we used the costume from Marvel Studios' *Avengers: Endgame*. For Kate's costume, we had to build a new costume because it would not have fit Hailee in a pleasant way. So we ▶

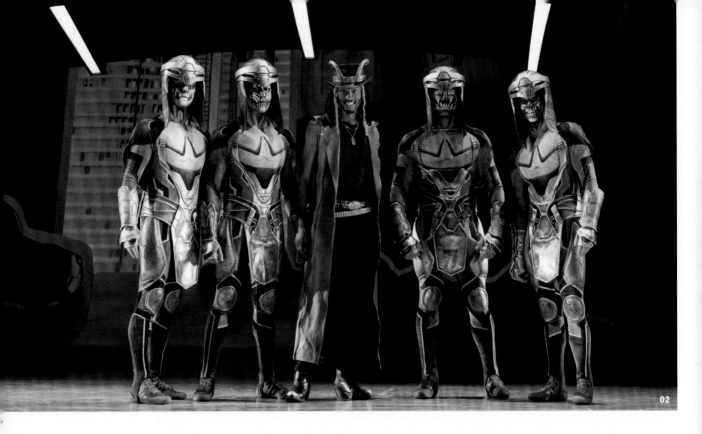

02

> ## "[Kate's] idea is that [Clint] needs something about his costume that stands out so he will appeal to people and be recognizable."

▶ recreated it to fit Hailee and added elements from the tuxedo she wore to that party. Then when Grills acquires the Ronin suit, that is a slightly smaller version of the costume to feel a little smaller on that character, and we added elements of the LARPing costumes to soften the Ronin costume and make it a little more humorous.

Can you talk about Eleanor Bishop's look?
Vera and I emailed back and forth before she came for a fitting, talking about design elements and what would look best on her character. We also talked about brands that we thought would work well with the character.

We ended up making pants for her from a pair of pants that she loves in her personal life that worked really well for the character. We copied them in rich burgundies and greens and camels. We also talked about keeping her fairly monochromatic and simple in silhouette.

She walks in in the red gown in the first episode and steals the focus of the room, which was the point of that dress. Then, in the sixth episode, when she enters the party in her green gown, we know about the darkness in her life. I wanted to show that with the color of that dress. There are elements of both light and dark throughout her costumes.

Then there's Jack Duquesne.
I played with a little bit of a playboy vibe for him with the turtlenecks and the plaid blazers and the polo shirts. I wanted him to feel sophisticated, because I felt like that is something that Eleanor would be attracted to. But I wanted him to feel playful and a little off at the same time. Tony definitely brought that to the character.

How did you want to represent Yelena?
There was a style of illusion on Yelena, for sure. We ended up with a costume that, in ways, is very similar to the white Widow costume she wears in the *Black Widow* film. In silhouette and in construction, we used a lot of the same types of materials, although we made it more stealthy, being black. And we added Black Widow style lines to the vest that replaced the green vest that she wore in the movie.

Then for her street wear, we tried to find elements that were quirky and interesting. I talked to the designer that created her final look for *Black Widow*. And I talked to Florence about how she saw this character evolving in street wear. We really wanted to find some unusual, funky pieces that made it feel [as if there was] an Eastern European influence to her fashion.

Yelena also has a striking green coat in the final episode…
Yelena needed a coat that she wears over her stealthy Black Widow costume. I needed something that covered her from the neck to the floor because she has this tactical ▶

01 Hawkeye's new look is an adaptation of his previous costume.

02 Members of the *Rogers: The Musical* cast show off their costumes.

03 Kate Bishop's costume mirrors her mentor's.

outfit underneath. So we designed this wool coat. I picked the green color. It's a Christmas party, [so we] wanted to add a little bit of spice and color to her costume so she blended in with everyone else that was at the party.

How did the tracksuits come about?
There was a lot of discussion of, "Is it going look silly if they're all wearing the same tracksuit?" We did variations where they were all in different things. They were just in regular street clothes, or they were in different kinds of tracksuits, in different colors, different sportswear elements. We decided that didn't make them feel like a collective. And we really wanted them to feel like a gang or one entity.

We did add specific elements on Kazi's tracksuit. And Ivan's tracksuit is a different color from the rest of them but tied in by the striping elements on the sleeves and trousers. Rhys Thomas [director] wanted him to feel a little more menacing, especially given his size. It's also a callback to the comic, where Ivan is the only part of the Tracksuit Mafia that is in a different color.

How did you go about creating Maya Lopez's look?
Her costume in the comic books didn't lend itself to the season we were shooting in because it is kind of a crop top and sleeveless. So we took elements like the "starburst" element on her costumes from the comic books.

We also took elements of the bandage wrapping that she has in the comic books, as well as some of the feather elements and tried to incorporate those in her costumes so that we know who she is by looking at her. But we also made her feel a little more grounded.

We wanted her to feel tough and independent, but, again, we went back to the comic books and created style lines based on that costume. We needed sleeves, so we added those. But we took the [bandage] wrapping element, and added them, the texture, to the trousers.

We also wanted to bring the red out in that costume. Her costume in the comic books is largely black, but we already had Yelena in black and had several other characters that wear black throughout the series. So we really wanted to bring a pop of color to her costume.

How did you want to update the Kingpin's look?
We have the flashback in which we hearken back to the first season of *Daredevil*, which took place about the same time as the Battle of New York. It was fun to recreate that with Vincent D'Onofrio and talk to him about the textures and the decisions that went into those costumes originally.

For the present day scenes we had to build Vincent's body out to feel as massive as Kingpin is in the comic books. Vincent's always been amazing as this character. But to be able to then add the mass and really create the character that's in the comic books added another level onto that performance that we were all excited about.

There were a couple of comic book covers and illustrations that we zeroed in on as looks that we wanted to build on. We settled on the white suit and the Hawaiian shirt, which worked brilliantly in the Polynesian restaurant setting.

Can you talk about those *Rogers: The Musical* outfits?
We talked about making a Broadway version of each of their costumes in a more elaborate way, but it started feeling a little cheesy. So we dialed it back. I think up until we saw all the actors together on stage performing there were concerns, but it all came together so well. ☻

04 Kate in the adapted Ronin costume.

05 Clint Barton goes casual.

06 Eleanor Bishop makes an entrance in her scene-stealing red dress, alongside Jack Duquesne.

07 Yelena wears night vision goggles as a part of her tactical suit.

HEATHER QUINN
WRITER

As one of the writers behind Marvel Studios' *Hawkeye*, Heather Quinn was integral to developing the characters and breaking the story. She looks back on collaborating with the cast on the ever-evolving story.

Why were you so keen to take on the task of writing Marvel Studios' *Hawkeye* series?
I wanted to write within this universe for a few different reasons. I'd met a few of the people at Marvel Studios and kind of knew how they worked. That was super exciting. As far as Marvel Sudios' *Hawkeye*, I got very excited about Kate Bishop and bringing in this new female character that comes from these great comics that are snarky and fun. And then the tonal juxtaposition of that eager new kid hero becoming a hero. Then also getting to broaden and tell a lot of

story for Clint Barton that we really hadn't gotten to see in the movies. All of that was thrilling.

How did the creative process work in the Marvel Studios' writers room?
The way Marvel Studios is doing TV is different than I would say a traditional writers room. It works more like a features room. That said, you are breaking story together very closely with the producer at Marvel Studios. You're breaking story with them, together with a group - I think we had ten people—all trying to find the tone and the character and the overall shape.

I think one of the exciting things that's also challenging is that Marvel Studios really wants to stand by what they actually believe [and] the story that they're telling. So if you get to a point where we don't feel like we're finding it, then you just start over, which is kind of audacious, but I think also gets you further in terms of story. So there was ten of us for about ten months or close to a year. It was definitely a very collaborative group effort. Then episodes get broken up and then come back to the room.

The story for Marvel Studios' *Hawkeye* must have undergone many changes over the course of a year. How did it evolve?

I mean, the process of how much was changed and adjusted even just on set, but especially since back then... I think ideally the story becomes like a living thing where we know what it should be. But you kind of have to let it move and keep changing. Some of that comes from the studio. Some of that comes from the directors' insight. Some of that comes from the actors' notes, because they're actually inhabiting these people. So it does keep evolving. Also [with] scenes that have come about, the seed of where it came from was something very innocent or funny or kind of a joke or a lark at the time [and] now really belongs there. That's a fun part of the creative process.

01 A young Kate Bishop witnesses the battle of New York.

02 Kate Bishop dons Clint Barton's Ronin outfit.

03 Barton and Bishop take a break with Bishop's dog, Lucky.

04 Kate Bishop and her faithful friend, Lucky.

05 As well as drama and comedy, the show delivers the action that Marvel Studios' fans have come to expect.

06 Bishop and Barton in action.

▶ How much did you collaborate with Jeremy Renner during the writing process?

It's been incredible to get to work with that caliber of an actor. But I think that's a great example of [where] I have this story in my mind for a year and a half or so and I have this character that I'm trying to understand from my perspective. But he's on the inside. And so he speaks a lot about how he feels like his job is being a barometer of truth and that he can only really perform something well if it feels true to him. So we would work from there a lot.

It's like, if there's lines or a scene or especially an emotional turn and it doesn't feel true to him, then I think our attitude was to listen to that and try to find the truth. Because if it's not authentic in him, then I think the audience will not connect with the moment.

I mean, it was really such a privilege to get to work with him in that way and then try to find the story or the words or the dialogue that was more true. I think that there are a lot of scenes and moments that became richer and more poignant from going through that process.

How did you balance the comedy and drama in Kate's scenes with Jack?

I have to give Hailee a lot of credit for that. What I observed in her is that she really is trying to track why she's doing almost everything she's doing. What the emotional motive is under that. She navigates that really well. It helps her to find tone of how big or how small [to play it] or the warmth or humor… She's not hitting those moments all at the same tone, at the same frequency. There's a breadth to it, and so I think we identify with those feelings.

How did you find working with multiple directors?

Working with Bert & Bertie and Rhys was great. I just tried to sort of adjust to what they needed from me in that moment. I tried to observe what their dynamic was with the cast, their process… and then [figuring out] how I could step into that and help join and support whatever that was, be it rewrites on the spot or character notes or whatever else. I think some of that too was determined more by scene work too and just what they wanted for the story and finding all those different things.

What was the process involved in writing for Maya Lopez a deaf character?

I'm amazed by what Alaqua Cox brings to the role. I mean, it strikes me as heroic that she could just step into this and inhabit it so bravely, especially as it is her first role. I feel very humbled getting to write for her and also humbled because it was my first time writing for a deaf character. In the room, we had a lot of conversations,

"I'm amazed by what Alaqua Cox brings to the role... I feel very humbled getting to write for her."

and we worked with consultants. So I gained some knowledge, but it was also a privilege to get to work more closely with her. Not just with her, but also with the interpreters and the consultant and the translators who were rehearsing with them.

It was such an amazing process to find how can we write dialogue that feels true for her. And then also, kind of letting go of [the dialogue] in a different way because it's gonna be translated. We want it to be the best ASL line, but I'm not writing that line, right? That's a whole other kind of art.

Watching her performance, it continued to evolve. Then it was doing little tweaks and notes where we were starting to see what she was able to bring out and how to support that with language, how to support that with cues on the page.

Did you enjoy making last-minute script changes as the production went on?

It's funny. There is definitely pressure. There's a couple moments, specifically, that I can think of where we were in rehearsal rewriting in real time on stage while a hundred people were waiting to do their jobs... I felt the pressure [when] it's three o'clock in the morning and a director is like, "Can you give a better joke?" And I'm like, "I haven't slept in three weeks... you've gotten the best out of me already!" You know, there's the pressure of that kind of performance.

But it's exciting in that moment [when] you're really locked into many different people. It's a very poignant moment of filmmaking, right? Like, I'm sitting there with the directors, the producer, the actors, we're all trying to find this thing. It's pressure, and it's also exciting. And it is also just a unique contrast to development writing where you are so interior and usually alone and often it's such a quiet, introverted thing... I think some of those most crazy, chaotic moments, in a weird way, start feeding you because they're so exciting. ⬤

07 Clint Barton and Kate Bishop's relationship is the core of Marvel Studios' *Hawkeye*.

TRINH TRAN | BRAD WINDERBAUM

EXECUTIVE-PRODUCERS

Executive producers Trinh Tran and Brad Winderbaum were involved in developing Marvel Studios' *Hawkeye* right from the start. They recall how they helped shepherd the show to the screen, from early discussions on fleshing out Clint's story to working with writers and casting key roles.

06

What did you find most intriguing about the character of Clint Barton?

Trinh Tran: What really intrigued me about Clint is that he is a Super Hero without any superpowers. He's standing next to gods and suits of armor, but this guy is just like me and you.

Brad Winderbaum: Clint has always been the human face of the Avengers. He has a family. He's trying to be a dad. He's got a really stressful job. He has all these things about him that I think parallel a lot of people's true life experiences.

Trinh Tran: I remember the first conversation I had with Kevin Feige about Hawkeye. Actually, it was originally a Hawkeye film. We started talking about it when we were filming Marvel Studios' *Avengers: Endgame*. What drew me to the character is we hadn't gotten a chance to really tell the Clint Barton story in the *Avengers* movies. Endgame is when you really see that emotional journey that he started going through by losing his family in the Blip and then getting them

back and in between that time becoming Ronin. There's a lot of story that we needed to tell on Clint Barton's side. So when it was time to pick the next project, I was interested in exploring more about that character, as well as introducing the female version of Hawkeye in the comics, Kate Bishop.

What I wanted to explore in this particular series was the Matt Fraction version of Clint Barton who is a little bit of the reckless loner but so funny and quirky. And who else better to draw that out of him but Kate Bishop?

Why did you decide to make a six-hour series rather than a movie?

Trinh Tran: I remember sitting in the trailer as we were shooting Marvel Studios' *Avengers: Endgame* going, "There is so much great material from the comics. How am I gonna put this all in two hours?" We thought, well, if there's a lot more story to tell about these two Hawkeyes, why not move that project over to the

02   **03**

Disney+ platform so we can have a lot more time to explore those two characters?

What does Jeremy Renner bring to the character?
Trinh Tran: I love Jeremy to death. *Hawkeye* was the show [where] I really saw a different side of Jeremy. I think that was part of what I wanted to draw out of Clint Barton as well... Jeremy is talented in so many ways, and there's that side of him that is so much fun. It's so comedic, and you see that in the banter that he has with Kate Bishop.
Brad Winderbaum: It's amazing what happens when you let actors like Jeremy Renner really have the space to explore their character and their backstory.

How did you develop Kate Bishop's character?
Trinh Tran: What drew me to the Clint Barton version of Hawkeye is that he doesn't have any superpowers, and nor does Kate Bishop. She is just a young girl who aspired to be a Super Hero when she was eight years

old [and saw] what Clint Barton could do. That really inspired her to be like, "I can be like him. I just have to work hard." At a very young age she got really interested and wanted to start learning martial arts and archery. That sort of evolved to the Kate Bishop that we know in this series... A young female archer being mentored by Clint Barton and having them learn from each other.
Brad Winderbaum: [Clint's] relationship with Kate Bishop was a chance to really highlight what's actually important to this character.
Trinh Tran: The heart of the *Hawkeye* series is the dynamic between Clint Barton and Kate Bishop. It is what makes them so interesting to watch, and we really pulled the inspiration from the Matt Fraction comic runs. It's about Clint and Kate and their nonstop bickering and bantering. Kevin and I had many discussions about [how] anything can happen in the background - there could be action and explosions and car chases and everything. But the forefront of it is their bond and their bickering.

01 Hailee Steinfeld goes before the camera as Kate Bishop.

02 Director Rhys Thomas takes Hailee Steinfeld through a scene.

03 The show takes time to explore the character of former Avenger Clint Barton.

04 Hailee Steinfeld and Vera Farmiga work on a scene while the hair and makeup team do their work.

"Hailee's an exceptional actress... She looked like the Kate Bishop that we had envisioned."

▶ **Hailee Steinfeld is perfectly cast as Kate Bishop...**
Trinh Tran: We had auditioned a few female actresses. We actually did a chemistry test with some of them with Jeremy one day. After looking at those auditions, it felt like it wasn't quite right. I think in the back of Kevin's mind, he had Hailee as Kate. And I think in seeing the auditions and trying to find other actresses to see if that would be the right fit, we actually just said, "Let's meet Hailee. Let's just have a conversation with her and see how that goes." Hailee's an exceptional actress. She has done many films and she looked like the Kate Bishop that we had envisioned.

I remember after the conversation, Kevin offered her the role right then and there. That was pretty remarkable. We came out of that meeting shaking her hand and going, "OK, you're in. You're gonna play Kate Bishop." I got super-excited and started getting all the comic package ready to go to give her.

How did you come to cast Alaqua Cox as Maya Lopez?
Trinh Tran When we started the casting process we wanted to make sure that we were looking into the deaf community to find that actress. We were looking into the Native American culture to make sure that we could get both a deaf and Native American actress. Now, when you put both of them together that way it's a massive undertaking to be able to find the perfect person to play Maya Lopez.

But Sarah Finn, our amazing casting director, who has cast all of our previous Avengers characters in the MCU, had a very challenging task. She cast a wide, worldwide search to find this character. We poured through so many tapes, and Alaqua, who came from Wisconsin, who is Native American, who is deaf, was just the perfect person to play this character. We saw her ambitious state of mind and how much she really was willing to push as far as she could in order to get Maya Lopez out to the world the way we envisioned her to be... Much like how I feel what this *Hawkeye* series represents is that anybody can be a Super Hero. All they have to do is work hard. We saw that in Alaqua. We saw how excited she felt [and] that she believed she was Maya Lopez. So, in turn, it's about taking chances on people. We took chances on a lot of our actors before, and we all felt that Alaqua was the right person to play Maya. ◉

01

02

THE DIRECTORS

Rhys Thomas and the duo Bert & Bertie were key to establishing Marvel Studios'
Hawkeye's winning combination of big laughs, heartfelt drama, and visceral action. The
three directors discuss their influences, the Marvel Studios way of working, and how they
went about throwing everything they could at their lead character.

03

What excited you the most about Marvel Studios' *Hawkeye*?

Rhys Thomas: I've always found Hawkeye compelling, especially the way that Jeremy has played him, because there's a sense of this ordinary guy driven by this sense of duty. He doesn't have the protection of superpowers, yet he runs into danger with the rest of them… I found it interesting that you get to join him in this place where, on the surface, he has found the peace that possibly he's always wanted. But you know there's been this price that's been paid.

Bertie: Before we even pitched on this, Trinh [Tran, producer] was talking about the tone of it. I think that's what really drew us to it—the fact that Clint Barton is going to be the "dad Clint Barton" and the Clint Barton of the Matt Fraction comics, and he has a hearing aid. Then you put into the mix this lively, super eager Kate Bishop. We were just like, that's a new tone. Marvel does tend to do this amazing action adventure tone but with comedy. But the comedy was really king in this one and

the absurdity. That speaks to everything that we love.

Rhys Thomas: When I first met with Trinh and talked to her about it, [she said] they wanted to be character based. There wasn't a big world-ending plot.

Bert: The hook for us was [also] bringing in a female Super Hero who isn't superhuman. Kate Bishop is amazingly skilled and as funny as anything. She is the heart and the comedy of this show for us.

What aspects of Hawkeye were you keen to explore?

Rhys Thomas: I enjoyed the humor and the tone. Matt Fraction's run of *Hawkeye* comics was definitely our baseline tonally, and that was a huge way in into thinking about what to do with this character. What I liked about Fraction, and I feel translates directly to Jeremy's version of Hawkeye, is he's a character that he has the weight of the world on his shoulders. He's this put-upon guy whose sense of duty or internal strength made him want to be part of the Avengers and stay with it… To constantly bring that guy up against too much energy and a situation that's out of his ▶

01 Directors Bert & Bertie pose with Hailee Steinfeld and Jeremy Renner.

02 Rhys Thomas and Hailee Steinfeld go over a scene.

03 The directors oversee an action-packed sequence with Steinfeld taking aim as Kate Bishop.

"When you have two characters that are so opposite in their energies, that's when it works."

▶ control and almost absurd in the twists and turns that it takes, that was entertaining to me. I thought the more we can throw at him and watch how he deals with it [the better]... There's so much story in Jeremy's face. Like, you just point a camera at him. You don't need to have him say anything. You know a lot of what's going on.
Bertie: We've seen *The Hurt Locker* Jeremy, the Jeremy of drama. And when we first started working on this show, we were doing the dramatic scenes quite a lot. There was a lot of him becoming Ronin again in New York. Then to see this levity and to see the comedy and how he improvised on top of the script and kind of made it better, we were all giggling behind the monitors.
Bert: What I enjoyed seeing him explore was the curmudgeonly Clint Barton. That's where the humor lies. It's a very comfortable space for him, but you can see over this time how that's grown and how he really mines it. That's the flipside to the Kate energy. When you have two characters that are so opposite in their energies, that's when it works.
Bertie: Then to see how capable Jeremy is physically... To watch that man sprint and to see the muscle memory and the techniques involved in [shooting a] left-handed arrow and then grabbing another. Everything's so on point with him.

How did you want to approach Kate Bishop?
Rhys Thomas: Through the writing process, I felt like one of the challenges was finding Kate's voice and trying to dial that in against Clint's. We knew we wanted to contrast her with Clint. You wanted this sort of classic buddy cop energy of these two divergent personalities meeting and to find that playfulness.

She's a younger character. She comes from wealth. She has a very different background to Clint... [But] you don't want her to sound too juvenile. You don't want her to sound too naïve. Finding that line where you could find that empathy was tricky. I feel like we went through quite a few different iterations of playing with that. It wasn't until Hailee came into the process and we saw her take these different elements, you suddenly realized, "We've over-thought this." She was that missing ingredient. She brought this grounded quality and had an intelligence that rounded off those edges that [we were] worried about.
Bertie: Hailee was incredible. She can run. She can fight. She was doing scenes opposite Fra Fee where she was punching, and you believed it. The archery coach was

04 Thomas goes over a scene with actress Vera Farmiga (right).

05 Bert & Bertie with Jeremy Renner.

06 Hailee Steinfeld, in Ronin gear, and Rhys Thomas.

07 Florence Pugh and Rhys Thomas on set.

08 Hailee Steinfeld and Bertie take a moment to discuss a low key scene.

blown away by how quick she picked all of this stuff up. She's a perfectionist off-screen, but on screen she just makes it so natural.

Rhys Thomas: A privileged character from New York can, on the surface, possibly be an unsympathetic character. Obviously we know that Kate has this traumatic backstory in losing her father and experiencing the Battle of New York. That was the thing: how do you bridge that? And Hailee, brings that kind of weight to it. That intelligence is always there, even if she's annoying Clint, even if she's seemingly flippant about a situation. You know that she's gonna come through this and she's gonna learn something. It was a big relief in those first few rehearsals with Hailee just to see, "Oh, this is who Kate is."

Bert: Her range is so great. She's so funny. She's so grounded. There's no point at which she's playing for the comedy. It's a challenging role to get right because of Kate's eagerness and also because of her privilege. She could tip into being the annoying whippersnapper quite easily, but [Hailee] has this wonderful vibrancy that she brings to it, which is super endearing.

How important was it to shoot in New York?

Rhys Thomas: It was important to go to New York because this is Clint's story and I was always interested in being able to ground this in a way. We don't have a fantastical story that takes us to outer space or these heightened locations. It's a very real experience and also a real time experience. So [we wanted] to get as much of the real texture and flavor of New York and the feeling of the different neighborhoods. The Downtown and Uptown contrast is hard to fake.

Bert: To get the scale and those vistas and the streets and the dirt and the texture and the colors and the people and the energy of New York was hugely important. I mean, Atlanta doubled a lot for what we needed it to, and it was incredible to film there. But New York is definitely a character in this show, so [we wanted to] submerge everyone into the world.

Bertie: We started filming in New York before anywhere else… It was a really great brain space for us to be in, which was like, "Ah, that's what the show is. That's where it's set."

What did Alaqua Cox bring to the show?

Rhys Thomas: I was lucky enough to have a hand in finding Alaqua and going through that casting process. Maya being Native American and deaf were both important elements of that character. But you're kind of looking for a needle in a haystack. It's not like you can cast a wide net. We met with a number of wonderful girls, some experienced, some not. But Alaqua just had this a grounded quality to her and a confidence… She just had this gung-ho quality that you don't really see. There was no sense of self consciousness.

Bertie: She's a role model, I have to say, for all of us. We cast Alaqua's cousin [Darnell Besaw] as young Maya. And Darnell and her mother and were talking about within their family, within the reservation, how much of a role model and a hero Alaqua is. Because she has overcome deafness and operations and losing a leg. She ▶

"Having a bad guy as good as the Kingpin is quite a delicious prospect."

▶ just came onto set and was like, "I'm ready and I'm available." She was so humble, but has great strength.

Rhys Thomas: Alaqua kicked ass!

Bertie: I remember we were talking about William [Lopez]'s death scene. And she was like, "Bertie, I don't think I've got the ability to cry on camera. I think the pressure will be too much." I was like, "No one has to cry in any given situation. We just have to show and feel the emotions." But we shot it and, just to show you how far she'd come, tears were rolling down that woman's cheeks. She was so in the moment.

The Tracksuit Mafia are great supporting villains.

Rhys Thomas: The references for me were *Die Hard* and *Lethal Weapon* and also '70s crime thrillers, going back to *Klute* and *The Conversation*. They all have this texture of these fringe characters that extend the life of the world of the show. So these guys were an opportunity to throw a different personality in front of Clint.

Bertie: The Tracksuit Mafia are not Chitari, are they? So it was really fun playing with. But there also needs to be a level of danger to them and unpredictability, which is where Kazi comes in. You don't know what he's going to do at any given moment and [there's] a depth and gravity to his character. But then you have the other Tracksuit Mafia who definitely bring some kind of light relief.

Bert: The best part about it is we actually got given tracksuits. Every Tuesday we had "tracksuit Tuesday" where we directed in character.

The Kingpin's return was a big surprise.

Rhys Thomas: Having a bad guy as good as Kingpin is quite a delicious prospect. When we started, there was almost a hesitation of giving too much and so we used him minimally. It was going to be this final reveal. But as we got further into it and as the story started evolving in post, we realized that there's a shadow that he cast just by the very nature of his character. The more that we could feel that and by tying him into Maya's story, it helped you understand that we were meddling in something bigger than just the Tracksuit Mafia.

Bertie: This is Fisk but at his lowest ebb, and there's a kind of a shame and a physical weight to him.

Rhys Thomas: Vincent had these very nuanced little touches that he brought to it, from his weirdly controllable twitch that he's able to send his face into when he's bottling up anger to playing with the cuff link.

09

It was fun to enhance them when we realized what a bigger part he was going to play.

How does Yelena fit into this world?

Rhys Thomas: In some ways, that was difficult—you know, it's someone else Clint's pissed off! How do you make that story different? But what's fun is you're bringing someone like Florence who has done such an amazing job of defining the Yelena character in Black Widow. Then she arrives on your set as this evolved character. It makes you realize what a universe it is. And [Florence] knows the way that Yelena talks and walks, so you've got that shortcut. Yes, it's a revenge story. But Florence has such a light energy to her and a twinkle in her eye. The weighty stuff is there but she has a real matter-of-fact way of playing it off as Yelena that keeps an energy to the show and brings in an interesting dynamic with Kate as well.

Bert: There's a great scene in Kate's apartment. When you have two great actors, sometimes the best thing to do is just let them sit down and talk.

How did you want to approach the action scenes?

Rhys Thomas: I wanted us to approach the action in a more practical way and not betray gravity or get too showy. I like the idea that you're with Clint and these guys and you feel it. When he gets hit, we really wanted to create the sense that you know he's getting hurt, that he's not a guy that can take a pounding and keep getting up. Every move he makes has a price. Heidi [Moneymaker] did a great job of choreographing those fights with that in mind.

Bert: The stunt team are the heart of the show. I think [Heidi's] bravery in what she created in the stunts is something we haven't seen before... the creativity, the humor that they included in their stunts.

Bertie: You give her the beginnings of an idea, and then she'll come back with a stunt viz that is worthy of multi-million dollar movies. Not just that, but there's a quirk to it. There's a real voice to what she gives you. It's not just action for action's sake, it's creative choreography with little character moments.

What did you enjoy the most about this series?

Bert: Blowing things up!

Rhys Thomas: I really enjoyed figuring out this world and casting these characters. Just having that different end point for Jeremy and wanting to ground that character was a fun baseline. I was stepping into [what] feels a little like a family. Almost every department head that we dealt with had experience with Marvel... Everyone could summon this bench of knowledge about how something was done.

Bertie: There's a Marvel way of working, and it means that you can always change things for the better. Like, don't be scared to throw in an idea last minute that will change something. We're meticulous planners, but there's a liberation with Marvel because they really are like, "How could this be better?" Out of that playfulness comes really special stuff. ◉

09 Bertie and Hailee Steinfeld prepare for a take.

MARVEL STUDIOS LIBRARY

MOVIE SPECIALS
- MARVEL STUDIOS' *SPIDER-MAN FAR FROM HOME*
- MARVEL STUDIOS' *ANT-MAN AND THE WASP*
- MARVEL STUDIOS' *AVENGERS: ENDGAME*
- MARVEL STUDIOS' *AVENGERS: INFINITY WAR*
- MARVEL STUDIOS' *BLACK PANTHER* (COMPANION)
- MARVEL STUDIOS' *BLACK WIDOW*
- MARVEL STUDIOS' *CAPTAIN MARVEL*
- MARVEL STUDIOS: THE FIRST TEN YEARS
- MARVEL STUDIOS' *THOR: RAGNAROK*
- MARVEL STUDIOS' *AVENGERS: AN INSIDER'S GUIDE TO THE AVENGERS' FILMS*
- MARVEL STUDIOS' *THE FALCON AND THE WINTER SOLDIER*
- MARVEL STUDIOS' *WANDAVISION*

MARVEL STUDIOS' LOKI: THE OFFICIAL MARVEL STUDIOS COLLECTOR SPECIAL

MARVEL STUDIOS' ETERNALS: THE OFFICIAL MOVIE SPECIAL

MARVEL STUDIOS' SPIDER-MAN NO WAY HOME: THE OFFICIAL MOVIE SPECIAL

MARVEL STUDIOS' DOCTOR STRANGE IN THE MULTIVERSE OF MADNESS: THE OFFICIAL MOVIE SPECIAL

MARVEL LEGACY LIBRARY

MARVEL'S AVENGERS BLACK PANTHER: WAR FOR WAKANDA: THE ART OF THE EXPANSION

MARVEL'S CAPTAIN AMERICA: THE FIRST 80 YEARS

MARVEL: THE FIRST 80 YEARS

MARVEL'S DEADPOOL: THE FIRST 60 YEARS

MARVEL'S FANTASTIC FOUR: THE FIRST 60 YEARS

MARVEL'S SPIDER-MAN: THE FIRST 60 YEARS

MARVEL CLASSIC NOVELS
- **WOLVERINE** WEAPON X OMNIBUS
- **SPIDER-MAN** THE DARKEST HOURS OMNIBUS
- **SPIDER-MAN** THE VENOM FACTOR OMNIBUS
- **X-MEN AND THE AVENGERS** GAMMA QUEST OMNIBUS
- **X-MEN** MUTANT EMPIRE OMNIBUS

NOVELS
- **MARVEL'S GUARDIANS OF THE GALAXY** NO GUTS, NO GLORY
- **SPIDER-MAN MILES MORALES** WINGS OF FURY
- **MORBIUS** THE LIVING VAMPIRE: BLOOD TIES
- **ANT-MAN** NATURAL ENEMY
- **AVENGERS** EVERYBODY WANTS TO RULE THE WORLD

- **AVENGERS** INFINITY
- **BLACK PANTHER** WHO IS THE BLACK PANTHER?
- **CAPTAIN AMERICA** DARK DESIGNS
- **CAPTAIN MARVEL** LIBERATION RUN
- **CIVIL WAR**
- **DEADPOOL** PAWS
- **SPIDER-MAN** FOREVER YOUNG
- **SPIDER-MAN** KRAVEN'S LAST HUNT
- **THANOS** DEATH SENTENCE
- **VENOM** LETHAL PROTECTOR
- **X-MEN** DAYS OF FUTURE PAST
- **X-MEN** THE DARK PHOENIX SAGA
- **SPIDER-MAN** HOSTILE TAKEOVER

ART BOOKS
- *THE GUARDIANS OF THE GALAXY* THE ART OF THE GAME
- *MARVEL'S AVENGERS: BLACK PANTHER: WAR FOR WAKANDA* THE ART OF THE EXPANSION
- *MARVEL'S SPIDER-MAN MILES MORALES* THE ART OF THE GAME
- *MARVEL'S AVENGERS* THE ART OF THE GAME
- *MARVEL'S SPIDER-MAN* THE ART OF THE GAME
- *MARVEL CONTEST OF CHAMPIONS* THE ART OF THE BATTLEREALM
- *SPIDER-MAN: INTO THE SPIDER-VERSE* THE ART OF THE MOVIE
- *THE ART OF IRON MAN* THE ART OF THE MOVIE

STAR WARS LIBRARY

STAR WARS: THE MANDALORIAN GUIDE TO SEASON ONE

STAR WARS: THE MANDALORIAN GUIDE TO SEASON TWO

STAR WARS: THE EMPIRE STRIKES BACK: THE 40TH ANNIVERSARY SPECIAL EDITION

STAR WARS INSIDER: THE FICTION COLLECTION VOLUME 2

STAR WARS: THE SKYWALKER SAGA THE OFFICIAL COLLECTOR'S EDITION

- *ROGUE ONE: A STAR WARS STORY* THE OFFICIAL COLLECTOR'S EDITION
- *ROGUE ONE: A STAR WARS STORY* THE OFFICIAL MISSION DEBRIEF
- *STAR WARS: THE LAST JEDI* THE OFFICIAL COLLECTOR'S EDITION
- *STAR WARS: THE LAST JEDI* THE OFFICIAL MOVIE COMPANION
- *STAR WARS: THE LAST JEDI* THE ULTIMATE GUIDE
- *SOLO: A STAR WARS STORY* THE OFFICIAL COLLECTOR'S EDITION
- *SOLO: A STAR WARS STORY* THE ULTIMATE GUIDE
- THE BEST OF *STAR WARS INSIDER* VOLUME 1

- THE BEST OF *STAR WARS INSIDER* VOLUME 2
- THE BEST OF *STAR WARS INSIDER* VOLUME 3
- THE BEST OF *STAR WARS INSIDER* VOLUME 4
- *STAR WARS:* LORDS OF THE SITH
- *STAR WARS:* HEROES OF THE FORCE
- *STAR WARS:* ICONS OF THE GALAXY
- *STAR WARS:* THE SAGA BEGINS
- *STAR WARS* THE ORIGINAL TRILOGY
- *STAR WARS:* ROGUES, SCOUNDRELS AND BOUNTY HUNTERS
- *STAR WARS:* CREATURES, ALIENS, AND DROIDS
- *STAR WARS: THE RISE OF SKYWALKER* THE OFFICIAL COLLECTOR'S EDITION

- *STAR WARS: THE MANDALORIAN:* GUIDE TO SEASON ONE
- *STAR WARS: THE MANDALORIAN:* GUIDE TO SEASON TWO
- *STAR WARS: THE EMPIRE STRIKES BACK* THE 40TH ANNIVERSARY SPECIAL EDITION
- *STAR WARS: AGE OF RESISTANCE* THE OFFICIAL COLLECTORS' EDITION
- *STAR WARS: THE SKYWALKER SAGA* THE OFFICIAL COLLECTOR'S EDITION
- *STAR WARS INSIDER: FICTION COLLECTION* VOLUME 1
- *STAR WARS INSIDER PRESENTS: MANDALORIAN SEASON 2* VOLUME 1
- *STAR WARS INSIDER PRESENTS: MANDALORIAN SEASON 2* VOLUME 2